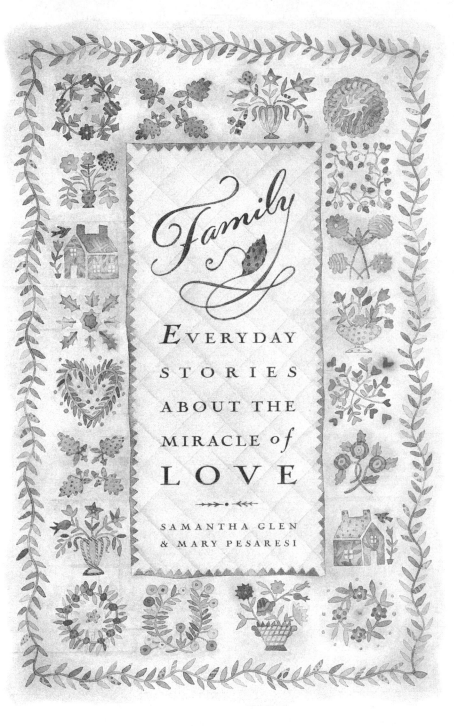

Family

EVERYDAY STORIES ABOUT THE MIRACLE of LOVE

SAMANTHA GLEN
& MARY PESARESI

PRIMA PUBLISHING

PRIMA PUBLISHING and colophon are registered trademarks of Prima Communications, Inc.

Library of Congress Cataloging-in-Publication Data
Glen, Samantha.
    Family : everyday stories about the miracle of love / Samantha Glen and Mary Pesaresi.
        p.   c.m.
    ISBN 0-7615-0615-2
    1. Family—Case studies.   I. Pesaresi, Mary.   II. Title
HQ518.G58   1996
306.85—dc20   96-28164
                                                                    CIP

96 97 98 99 00 01 AA 10 9 8 7 6 5 4 3 2 1
Printed in the United States of America

How to Order
Single copies may be ordered from Prima Publishing, P.O. Box 1260BK, Rocklin, CA 95677; telephone (916) 632-4400. Quantity discounts are also available. On your letterhead, include information concerning the intended use of the books and the number of books you wish to purchase.

Visit us online at http://www.primapublishing.com

To Alan,

my helpmate,

my best friend,

my inspiration,

my greatest love.

—Samantha

To Joe,

my dearest life's partner;

To Sara and Anne,

my most precious treasures;

To Mom and Dad,

my best loving teachers.

—Mary

>>> • <<<

We dedicate this

book to you.

— CONTENTS —

CONTENTS

CONTENTS

– ACKNOWLEDGMENTS –

IN KEEPING WITH THE SPIRIT OF THIS BOOK, WE BLESS THE DAY WE MET OUR husbands, Alan Glen and Joe Pesaresi. Their support, encouragement, love, wonderful meals to sustain us (Alan), and proofreading into the night (Joe), made it all worthwhile.

Sara and Anne—our wise little girls—delighted in our stories, and were (almost always) ungrudging of the time Mom and Samantha spent with their computers instead of with them.

Everybody made this truly a family project.

Every contributor to this book knows how we feel about them, yet we want to say it one more time. We appreciate your stories, laughter, tears, and smiles. We are grateful for your interest, which led us to scrutinize every detail. Your comments welled from the deep caring you brought to this project. This book is yours as much as ours.

We must thank Georgia Hughes, our editor, for her infinite patience, and a graciousness under pressure that make her a joy with whom to work. And Georgia, we also appreciate your superb eye. You kept us focused. Betsy Towner, our project editor, with her unending enthusiasm and teamwork, brought a true love of family to the book.

What can we say about Meredith Bernstein, the best agent in New York, who is so much more than our representative? Bless your gifts of faith, style, and friendship.

Greg Aaron was the first to inspire us, and to believe others would love these stories. We won't forget your help in bringing this book into being.

And Linda Azar . . . a special sister. Not only do you have a poet's soul, you weave a story like a dream. For your calming influence, your critical eye on the page, and especially your writing, we're more than glad you were an integral part of this project.

— STRAIGHT FROM THE HEART —

WHEN WE WERE CHILDREN, WE ENGAGED IN THE NEVER-ENDING DELIGHT of skipping stones in still ponds, watching the rippling circles grow wider and wider until they lapped the shore and tickled our bare feet.

The pebble we tossed many months ago was the idea for a book to celebrate those whom we too often take for granted: our families. The resultant ripples extended farther than we dreamed, and touched people in ways we couldn't have imagined.

Word spread, stories flooded in—not just from acquaintances and family, but from folks who introduced themselves as a friend of a friend, or a stranger who had heard through some mysterious grapevine about our project.

All contributors wanted to share a personal incident or reflection that honored those close to them. In telling their tales, they were deeply affected in ways that took them and us by surprise.

Time and again, people told us, "I've wanted to talk to my mom (or dad, brother, friend) about how much she meant to me, but I never seemed to find the right moment." Others wept as their memories unfolded because old wounds had never been closed. But many were surprised to discover peace in the sharing, and some have begun to heal. Other irrepressible spirits found laughter the best medium to pay tribute.

Without exception, the storytellers revised and edited their memories, determined to get the facts straight, the emotions correct. And by so doing they enriched the humor, drama, or poignancy of the narratives. As their stories passed back and forth from us to them, a flow of empathy grew with every one of the tale weavers. Their openness touched us. The protective pride they felt toward their remembrances inspired us to strive to write their stories with the same truth, passion, mirth, or pathos with which they recounted them.

The tales evolved into their own life's lessons, each memory a message, each recollection an acknowledgment of the intensity of love, faith, trust, and hope that exists in our lives.

And we came to understand the many versions of family in this mosaic we call America. This book celebrates our diversity, in all its cultures, creeds, colors, and circumstances. Its vignettes bear testament to the varied attitudes, mores, and values that have shaped the way we live today. It speaks with the candor of youth, the industry of middle age, and the wisdom of our elders.

Every contributor, unless they desired otherwise, is recognized at the beginning of each story. A few of the narrators have written their tales themselves, generously allowing us to edit. Others related their yarns, granting us the honor of writing them and trying to do them justice. To every one of these folks, we say thank you. Knowing you is a privilege.

This book has touched our souls. We hope that by sharing the comforting gestures, unselfish acts, loving rituals, and caring words that are the weft and weave of its stories we can remember that most people in the world are decent human beings; rejoice in the goodness that surrounds us; and understand the power of even our smallest action to influence the lives of those we hold most dear.

So we present a glad tribute—straight from the heart—to the parents, grandparents, siblings, cousins, aunts, uncles, and friends who help us make it through our days and nights, and bind up the threads of our lives.

Ties That Bind

The greatest happinesses are family happinesses

—Dr. Joyce Brothers

Matchbox Cars

From K. *Neal Smith, 36, consultant*

ᘓᘓᘓᘓ

*L*IFE WAS PRETTY IDYLLIC IN THE SOUTHERN CALIFORNIA of the early 1970s—unless, like me, you happened to be the youngest of three boys in a family of seven.

Our house was the second from the end on a cul-de-sac that backed up against a grand expanse of parkland through which the kids biked home after school. From our kitchen window, you could see the playground with its swings and slides, seesaws, and giant jungle gym.

I loved that playground. It was an extension of our own backyard, and my mother would let me go play there a couple afternoons a week by myself. This was eminently practical, since my mother had her hands full with three boys and four girls.

Byron and Doug wanted nothing to do with their kid brother, and I guess I couldn't blame them. There were nine years between Byron and me, and I was seven years younger than Doug. "Go away. Get out of here!" they'd yell, if I so much as put my head around the corner of the garage while they were playing basketball with their friends.

Older brothers being older brothers, Byron and Doug thought it was their duty to give me a bad time. They would trip me up in the hallway to see if I would cry. If Mom said they had to keep an eye on me, they'd figure out some way to torment me.

When I was about five, they stuck me in my old baby buggy to take me for a ride. It was a bulky European contraption with springs, and a bonnet that was hinged in the middle so you could swing it back and forth to shade the baby. It was huge inside, easily big enough for a five-year-old.

We were having a fun game. My brothers had tied a rope to the handles of the baby buggy and were pulling me up and down our cul-de-sac. This was perfectly safe because no cars ever seemed to drive down our road, and I was too happy to be playing with Byron and Doug to care. But all of a sudden, my two hellion siblings froze, a look of comic horror on their faces. "There's a car coming, a car coming!" they screeched, and let go of the rope.

I didn't think to listen for the sound of a motor. I didn't think to remember that even though my brothers may have teased me day and night, they would never deliberately put me in danger. My five-year-old sensibilities registered only one emotion: terror!

I pushed upward to jump out of the rolling carriage, but the ancient perambulator had seen better days. A sinister rip of cloth reverberated through the quiet of the afternoon as the bottom split open under my weight and my two chubby legs hit the ground. Next thing I knew, I was a living brake to a runaway pram.

My brothers, of course, thought it was the funniest thing they'd ever seen, and they didn't stop laughing for a good ten minutes. I felt silly and wished I hadn't screamed so loud.

"It's all right, kid," Byron said, trying to keep a straight face while he surreptitiously checked me over to make sure I was okay.

Then my two brothers strolled back into the house, leaving me in the middle of our driveway with my backside stuck in the buggy.

I was mad but not hurt, and I still looked up to them in awe, as younger brothers are wont to do. Besides, I could always retreat to my own secret world—the world of my Matchbox cars.

Oh, how I loved my Matchbox cars. They were the pride of my life, the Snoopy blanket of my existence. I would play for hours in the middle of the living room floor, my two-inch miniatures forming a sacred circle around me.

There was the green construction crane that I could crank up and down so that its painted teeth would open like the real thing; the shiny blue Cadillac with the 1950s fins and doors that really opened; the gleaming red fire engine with the detachable ladder.

I was always very careful to gather every last one of my trucks, police cars, vans, and engines and pack them in their blue and yellow carrying case. I wasn't going to risk any chance that Byron or Doug would step on my cherished replicas with their oversized PF Flyers. To them, my passion was kid's stuff.

It wasn't my habit to play with my Matchbox cars out of the house, but in the spring of my sixth year, one glorious April Saturday, Mom wanted to vacuum. So I toted my precious case to the park until she would call me home. I avoided the playground because it was crowded with kids. Instead I found a flat piece of stubby grass under a maple tree green with new leaves, and settled in for a blissful two hours.

"Whatcha got there?"

I didn't have to look up to know whose shadow had darkened the sun. Jonas Arbnuth was two grades ahead in school, and it was usually beneath his contempt to bother me. But I was alone, and he obviously hadn't dealt his ration of torment for the day.

Jonas was a short, squat kid with premature acne that pocked his face with pinprick bubbles of white matter. It made him look even uglier than his reputation. He was the bully whom every smaller child feared. When Jonas Arbnuth tripped you, he followed it up with a nasty kick. When Jonas Arbnuth demanded the ransom of your school lunch, you surrendered your sandwich and retreated as fast as your legs could pump out of his sight.

Now the dreaded bully towered above me, and all I could focus on was the black striped T-shirt that rode up above his dimpled belly button. I was vaguely aware that there was another boy with him, his latest toady, a new kid I didn't know much about.

"Whatcha looking at, skinny? Cat got your tongue? I asked you what you got there."

I slammed my case shut.

"Hey, me and Mickey just want to look," Jonas wheedled.

"Come on, let's see. They look kinda cool," Mickey added.

The two boys hunkered down either side of me like jailers. I opened my blue and yellow case as slowly as I could.

"So take 'em out. What are you, chicken?"

I was scared, but I was proud of my cars. For some reason I'll never understand, I chose my favorites, the red fire engine and the blue Cadillac, and held them palms up so they could see.

Jonas was fast. He grabbed my red fire engine and blue Cadillac, dangling them out of my reach. "Typical kid's stuff. What do you think, Mickey?"

"Please give them back."

"Oh yeah, you want 'em back? Whatcha got to give?"

"I don't have anything, but I will tomorrow."

"Now or never."

Before I could plead any more, Jonas and Mickey were up and laughing. "See ya, sucker," they called over their shoulders as they sauntered away.

I was crying when I ran into the house. I burst into the kitchen. "Mom, Mom, they took my car, they took my fire engine, they took—" *Where was Mom?*

Instead, Byron and Doug were parked in the kitchen, their lips fastened to the open mouths of two Coke bottles. "Who took what? What happened?"

I was having trouble getting the words out, my brothers looked so stern. I held out my Matchbox case. "Jonas and Mickey, from school, they took my—"

Byron glanced at Doug. Doug glanced at Byron. "What'd they look like, which way'd they go?" my older brothers demanded.

Have you ever seen two greyhounds exit the gate when the rabbit's let loose? Well, Byron and Doug were built as lean and muscled as any cool teenagers, and took off so fast I thought they could've outrun a greyhound any day.

They were back in less than fifteen minutes, strolling into the family room as I was explaining to Mom for the second time what had happened.

Without a word, my brothers opened my blue and yellow case. With extraordinary care, they deposited my red fire truck and my blue Cadillac back in their proper compartments. Then, as if nothing out of the ordinary had happened, they headed back to the kitchen to continue their customary three o'clock raid on the refrigerator.

I followed my heroes. "Wow. Thanks Byron. Thanks Doug."

My brothers ignored me, as was their habit. I persisted, as usual. "You saved my cars, you—"

Doug swung around and gave me his best mean-brother look. "This doesn't change anything, kid. We're still gonna mess with you if we feel like it."

"Yeah, but nobody else better try," Byron finished for him.

With that, they turned their backs on me and resumed the important task of gathering the necessities for a three-tier sandwich.

They were right. It didn't change our relationship or make anything different. After all, it was only fitting that brothers give brothers a bad time now and again. But if I wasn't old enough to guess before, I knew now how Byron and Doug really felt. For all their posturing, all the tricks they played—they loved me.

>>> • <<<

Doug now owns a children's clothing company in San Diego. Byron is a tax attorney in Utah. All three brothers are close and see each other often. And Neal still has his Matchbox cars.

As Long As They Have Need

From Sunny Mendelson, 30s, marketing director

⟨⟨⟨⟨⟨⟨⟨

$\mathcal{I}$ WATCHED FROM MY FRONT LAWN AS MY NEXT-DOOR neighbors, Michele and Randy Williams, climbed from their black Jaguar. Michele disappeared into the back seat, fussing over something. When she reappeared, she was holding a bundle of fluffy blue and white blankets. "Sunny, come see," she called. She lifted the blanket, and revealed a wrinkled, red-faced baby. "It's a boy, Sunny," she whispered.

I didn't quite know who was more beautiful—my proud friend, with her golden hair swept back from her delicate features, or the innocent in her arms, and I said so.

"Don't be silly," Michele chided. She tickled his plump little belly and let her fingers trace his perfect rosebud mouth. "Look at him, he's precious."

"Yes! Yes," I cried in surrender, "he's gorgeous."

Randy just grinned, then held the door for his wife and beckoned me to follow.

A deep-blue, velvety pram stood proudly in their magnificent foyer. Through carved double doors, I could glimpse the familiar elegant rooms, inviting in muted pastels, shining brass, and gleaming hardwoods—*House Beautiful* in living color.

"Quite a first home for a kid," I observed.

Michele laughed. "What does he care? All he wants is to be fed and loved. Don't you, precious?"

"I'll hold him," Randy said. He cradled the boy in his hands, and gazed at him for a tender moment. "He's a fine one." The man snuggled the tiny form against his chest as his fingers stroked the downy head. "*This* is satisfaction."

"He's what, your fourth? I'd think you two might have gotten used to the baby thing by now."

Michele tiptoed and kissed the child on his forehead. "Never."

I left and went back to my gardening. But I could imagine the routine next door: Lights would be on all hours of the night; Michele would walk the floor, cradling a fitful baby against her heart. I could almost hear her humming her favorite songs from the *Sound of Music*.

I admire those two. I couldn't do it. You see, I have no children at home. But then, neither do Randy and Michele. They are childless. This little boy is not their baby, and never will be. My neighbors are volunteer foster parents for an adoption agency—temporary Mom and Dad—although there is nothing temporary about the couple's love for these babies.

I have watched it take months for my friends to be approved for their volunteer duties; seen them attend courses, provide references, allow security checks of their home. All this for a twenty-four-hour-a-day job that pays bupkiss.

Michele insists, "Whatever I have to do is fine."

At last, the babies came. The infants my friends choose to cherish are like all newborns: some a bit colicky, some high-strung, some sleepless, some no trouble at all. And like all newborns, they crave a full measure of love and attention. It's their good fortune to land, at least for a moment, in the arms of Michele and Randy, who dispense without stint the tender rituals of new parents—bathing, diapering, feeding, cuddling.

I visited Michele one afternoon before Randy was home from work, and was greeted by fretful crying coming from the kitchen. My friend was attempting to feed her son of the moment. Her natural bloom was gone in cheeks turned to chalk, and dark circles made her tired eyes look enormous. She'd been up day and night for weeks with this infant, who seemed to absorb love and time like a thirsty man does water. But she didn't complain. This little boy needed her as much as those before him.

What was causing her distress today was the news that the baby's mother had disappeared without signing any adoption papers. If the woman didn't return, the child would be placed in the county foster care system.

"I understand that poor lady's stress," Michele said, "but this baby needs a permanent home. He shouldn't get too used to me." She stroked his round, little cheek, just a caress with her fingertips. "Don't cry now," she soothed. "I'll take care of you."

The little one calmed at her voice. I couldn't see my friend's face, but the infant's eyes held such a look of total adoration that I had to turn away. For those two, no one else in the world existed at that instant. I had always known of the hardships, but now, in that baby's face, I saw and understood the immeasurable rewards of Michele's labors. Luckily, the mother returned, and there proved to be no obstacles to stop the adoption.

Michele and Randy live for the moment with each baby—sometimes for two months, sometimes three—before the agency is on the phone again. The message is always the same. The new parents are processed, and eager for their child. My friends have only a few days before they say good-bye. Now the bittersweet ride on an emotional roller coaster begins.

"I never cry in front of the new parents when I give them their baby," Michele says. "It's the happiest day of their lives."

My neighbors come home rent with both satisfaction and loss. They know the infant is now with wonderful parents, but that means there is no warm, tiny presence sleeping in the nursery, no little fingers holding tight to their hands, no squeals of delight or cries of alarm. Michele will move a cushion and find a pacifier, or pick up discarded clothes and smell a lingering baby fragrance. Then tears she has managed to hold start to flow.

The couple have marvelous memories as solace. Scattered about their home are framed pictures in silver and gold—each of their "children," forever frozen in infancy. Often the new parents will send pictures and letters describing the babies in their different stages of growth. The couple rejoice over them and relish each bit of information. And Michele and Randy have each other. It's where they gather their strength.

When I ask Michele how she can go through this time after time, she explains, "I'll do it again and again and again as long as they need me. Whatever we give, we get back so much more. Believe me, the joy far outweighs the pain."

Michele and Randy provide something crucial for these babies at the critical first moments of life: unconditional love and caring. And watching them all these years, I've learned that striving to be recognized, to make a name for yourself, isn't what life's all about. It's what you do for others in this world that matters. Michele and

Randy send these babies into life with love, and because of their efforts these little ones, who might have fallen through the cracks of an imperfect system, have a fine chance for a good life.

→→→• ←←←

Randy is a builder and developer. When she's not caring for babies, Michele is a flight attendant for American Airlines. Before becoming a world-class foster mom for the Barker Foundation in Cabin John, Maryland, she lent her volunteer services to hospital boarder babies (infants abandoned at the hospital).

Grandmother's Eyes

From S. C. Chazen, 60s, clinical social worker

꧁꧂

IN MY FAMILY HANUKKAH IS THE MOST IMPORTANT CELEBRATION of the year. People come from all over the country for this, our biggest family gathering.

The tradition in our home was started more than sixty years ago by my mother, Anna. On the first night of Hanukkah, we would light a candle, and one of us was chosen to recite the ancient story of the miracle of the oil that lasted eight days. The tale was retold, and a new candle lit every evening, until the menorah was blazing.

My mother made this holiday magical. Her table shone with silver and damask, fragrant with flowers. Anna used to make all the decorations herself, and each night there was a small, beribboned package next to the dinner plate of each of her three children. When we played the dreidel game, she would proffer a wealth of gold-foiled chocolate coins to be won or lost by the spin of the top.

These customs have continued throughout the years. We've grown, gone to college, married, had children of our own, but we always try to get home for Hanukkah. And the opening of the presents is special to all of us.

Last December Anna was ninety-two. She was surrounded by her children, grandchildren, and great-grandchildren—four generations, forty strong, gathered together for this most cherished of rituals. Sadly, my mother's vision has failed. She can see light and shadows, but can no longer distinguish faces or details. Anna was not able to see the gifts as they were being opened. She could hear the excitement, the paper unwrapping, but she couldn't participate.

Then I saw my daughter Kathy sitting beside Anna on the couch. I watched as she guided her grandmother's fingers over the paper and ribbons and helped her to unwrap her gifts. Kathy described the contents of each package, and held the presents up close so my mother could smell and touch them.

My other daughter, Louise, and my niece Suzy now joined them. Then each of Anna's eight grandchildren in turn brought the rest of the family's gifts over to her and played out the loving rite.

This small drama continued throughout the three hours of festivities. The children never left Anna's side. They could not and would not leave her out of the celebration.

The lingering shroud of sadness that had enveloped my mother all afternoon vanished. Anna sat up straight, as is her wont. The quick, birdlike movements of her head and hands, the flash of her smile, told me that once again she was part of the family's joy.

Whatever else my children may do in the future, this one shining gesture I will never forget. On this Hanukkah night, they were very special gift givers. For Anna, it was the gift of sight. For me, it was a confirmation that I had done something right in this life.

Anna still lives at home, with the company of a nurse. She loves to read—two books a week in Braille—and looks forward to the frequent visits of her family and friends. And they are always delighted to see her.

Cycles of Life

From Titana Mena Gargini, 27, homemaker, Isla Mujeres, Mexico
As told to and written by L.M. Azar, 40, poet

⟨⟨⟨⟨⟨⟨⟨

I WAS ABOUT EIGHT MONTHS PREGNANT WHEN MAMA ROSA got sick. We brought her from the island to our cousin's house in Merida to be near the doctors and hospitals. We all took turns caring for her. It was 'round-the-clock work to keep her comfortable and make sure she had all her medications.

I remember the contentment on Mama's face when she put her hands on my belly and talked to the baby inside me, telling her how much she loved her and what a wonderful life she was going to have. Her pain seemed far away when she was talking to the baby. She called her *mi corazoncita,* my little heart.

My husband, Gregorio, was worried about me. Many people here believe that a pregnant woman should not be close to the sick, for it could rob the life within. I tried to pay no attention to such beliefs. But sometimes, when I wasn't feeling well, I'd become worried. Then I would remember Mama's love and devotion, her sacrifices, how she sat up nights with her children and grandchildren when we were sick.

I became aware of the cycles of life, and how the new comes to replace the old. I prayed that my baby would have the wisdom and the goodness that were such a part of her grandmother.

Papa died just after I was born. He was gathering coconuts when one fell and hit him on the head, killing him. So Mama raised all six of us pretty much alone. She fed us by taking in laundry and selling her wonderful breads. My brothers fished and my sisters helped Mama bake. She was a clever woman and always seemed to find ways to make ends meet.

I remember once when our island was being evacuated because of an approaching hurricane. My brothers were out fishing, and Mama refused to leave. She was one of the last people remaining. She waited on the beach 'til returned.

But that is how she was. Her life was the family, and she loved to laugh and have a good time with all of us. So when Mama took ill, it was like the sunshine in our lives was fading. All we could do was make her last days as comfortable as possible.

Finally, I went into labor and Gregorio rushed me to the hospital. After what seemed forever, I delivered a beautiful baby girl. I'll never forget the moment the doctor gave me my baby to put to my breast. I thought of Mama and how she must have felt with each one of us, a love so big you feel like you will explode.

With my baby resting on my chest, I was overcome with joy, sadness, and an emotion I couldn't contain. My baby's first bath was of her mother's tears.

We rested in the hospital for several days, then Gregorio took me and the baby back to where Mama was quickly fading. I remember the first moment Mama laid eyes on my little angel, she said, "Oh, *mi corazoncita*, what a beautiful baby you are with the color of cinnamon." So we named the baby Canela, which means cinnamon. Mama was so pleased with her name.

It wasn't long after I brought the baby out of the hospital that we all packed up and returned to the island. The doctors didn't think Mama could make the seven-hour trip home by car and then boat, but we packed her oxygen tank and all her medicines and took her back to her beloved place of birth—the land she loved so much. Less than an hour after we arrived, Mama died. She was so happy because she had seen and held her grand-daughter, then returned home where she could rest in peace.

The people from the village marched with us to the cemetery. Every voice joined in song as we buried Mama. We put angels on her grave and built a small house where we placed flowers, candles, and special foods that Mama loved best.

Canela will know her grandmother through our words only, but with that knowledge she will continue on with the cycle of life.

→→→•‹‹‹

Titana and Canela visit Mama Rosa's resting place often, always taking a branch of fragrant jasmine to adorn her grave. And as Mama Rosa had predicted, Canela does have a wonderful life.

Coming Home

From Cathy Grant, 36, homemaker

I'VE ALWAYS CONSIDERED MYSELF A STRONG, INDEPENDENT female. But I didn't know the gut ache of aloneness until we moved to America.

It had been a big decision for my husband, two children, and me to pull up roots in Toronto, Canada, and emigrate. But Doug had a job offer he couldn't refuse—chief financial officer for a major company in northern Virginia. He'd signed on January first, and I was to follow as soon as possible.

We had two shocks in quick succession. The first was that within two weeks after Doug came on board, his new company entered into major merger talks with a competitor. That meant my husband accompanied the president all over the United States for the negotiations. His weekends were spent in New York or Wisconsin rather than at home with us. But in Canada, cushioned by old friends and some family, Doug's absences were not so bad.

Of course, I missed his smile, his jokes, his loving support. Of course, the kids went out of their skulls when he came home. But, caught up in the move and in good-byes, we were too busy to be lonely.

Once we got to Virginia, however, loneliness struck like a runaway train.

Then came the second shock. I'd been given rapturous accounts of the mildness of the weather compared to the snow-cold misery of the Toronto winters. Never believe propaganda, no matter how benign.

We arrived in March, during an ice storm that raged for five days, and Doug couldn't be home to welcome us. He was in New York.

So, here I was—up to my ying-yang in boxes, housebound kids, and a sick dog. I couldn't find anything. The electricity kept going out. Thank God, the Domino's Pizza guy managed to slog through the storm so I could feed the children. Even the dog had extra-cheese deep-dish that night. I saved the pepperoni for breakfast.

The phone rang at five o'clock. I dug through wadded up paper and piles of cardboard until I fished it out from behind my oh-so-empty canisters. "Hello?"

"Cath?"

"Yes, Doug, it's me. You were expecting maybe Michelle Pfeiffer?"

"A guy can hope, can't he?"

"Ha ha."

"You're in a good mood."

"Peachy."

"I just wanted to check in with you real quick, Cath, and see how your day's been, and how the kids are."

"Great," I answered . . . *if you consider two nutsy children, one dying dog, an ice rink for a driveway, and no heat great.* "The man brought the wood this morning."

"At least you can have a fire."

"Yep."

"I wish I were home. I hate being away from you, and I'm sorry you have to shoulder all the burden of the move."

My heart thawed. I knew he meant every word. "We miss you, too. Like crazy. But Doug, we both have jobs to do."

"I know. I know. Just a sec, someone's at the door." I waited, hearing snatches of conversation before my husband picked up the phone again. "Listen, honey, the limo's here. We're going out to Montrachet for dinner. I'll call you when I get back. I love you."

"Yeah. Love you, too."

The phone dangled from my fingers, and I caught a glimpse of my reflection in the black expanse of naked window over the kitchen sink. My short brown hair clung to my neck in greasy strings. I'd been wearing the same jeans and sweatshirt for two days. Dark smudges underlined my eyes, and my cheeks and lips were screaming for color. Try as I might, I could find neither hide nor hair of the girl Doug had fallen for—at first sight, he always said—so many years before.

I kicked at the Domino's box crumpled on the floor. No wonder I hardly saw my husband anymore. How could I compete with Montrachet and limousines?

Within minutes, the phone rang again. "Hello?" I mumbled, barely gathering the strength to be civil. If this was the power company calling with another excuse, I was going to lose it.

"Cath? It's Doug. I'm coming home."

Please, please. "You can't. The biggest ice storm of the century is raging out there."

"I can't take being away from you another day. And I've got to see the kids, I'll go crazy if I don't."

"But the merger talks . . . the negotiations." It would be business suicide for Doug to leave now. He hadn't established himself yet.

"I heard your voice, Cath. You sound like I feel. I'm coming home."

"I'm so glad." The last word ended in a squeaky sob. I swallowed hard and tried again. "I'll keep the fire burning."

"I know you will. I'll be home by seven."

At 6:30 both kids and I were groomed and ready for Doug. The fire was lit, and our new home was beautiful, painted in the delightful colors of anticipation.

Three hours later, I tucked two very disappointed little souls into bed, and settled by the fire to listen to the storm rage. *Why didn't I tell him to stay in New York? Why had I let him travel in this?*

At ten o'clock the phone rang, and I made a dive for it.

"I'm on the ground," Doug said. "Almost home, honey. See you in half an hour."

I threw two big logs on the fire. Was it my imagination, or had the wind picked up, howling like a banshee around the house? Were ice pellets truly trying to break our windows? My last fingernail was chewed to the quick, and I started in on the pencil I clutched.

By eleven my weary body didn't care that my heart was scared to death. I found myself dozing and starting, dozing and starting until finally, I fell asleep.

The next thing I knew, a pair of cold arms was wrapped around me. I felt the scratchy weave of a Fair Isle sweater against my cheek, and the sweet familiar scent of Drakkor Noir cut into my nightmares. I pushed my face deeper into the rough, wool haven of my husband's chest and inhaled deeply. We didn't move for a long time.

"I had to put the kids to bed," I whispered finally.

"Come on." Doug smiled and led me upstairs.

Mark and Jane were dead to the world. I watched my husband bend over each in turn. He rested his face ever so lightly against their cheeks and inhaled deeply.

"I love their smell. I'd almost forgotten it," he said, a little sheepishly.

We went downstairs again. The former owners had left a bright white light on the landing. For the first time, I took a good look at Doug's face. He's only forty, but in the wee hours of this morning, fatigue had fashioned his cheeks into sunken hollows. He looked like he'd been dragged through a knothole.

He was the most gorgeous sight I'd ever seen.

We didn't do anything grand the rest of the night—no storybook lovemaking on a bearskin rug. In our house it would more likely have been a pizza box anyway. I rummaged a blanket and pillows from some carton, and we snuggled together in front of the fire, not saying much. In fact, words were inadequate and unnecessary.

He left at 5:30 in the morning, and I stayed awake. All I thought about was my husband, and the efforts he'd made for only a few hours with us.

And I knew I was loved. And it was enough.

>>>• <<<

The merger went through and Doug is home more often. For Cath, her husband makes everything fall into place; he's the missing piece of the puzzle of her day. When they are together the whole family fits—the children, Doug, and Cath—whole and complete.

Follow Your Heart

What would life be if we had no courage to attempt anything?

—Vincent Van Gogh

It Was More Than Playing Streetball

From Mike Hayes, 32, stockbroker

꒰꒱꒰꒱

*W*HEN YOU'RE A KID, THE MOST IMPORTANT THING IN LIFE is to hang with the guys, to belong. In the summer of 1971, I was eight years old. And in my world, to belong meant to play streetball.

I lived in a close-knit community where the guys on my block had names like Popoli, Pachano, Romano, and Stellabuto. It was a place where an outsider who'd just moved in, and didn't know the rules, was actually stupid enough to slap a local girl. Big mistake. Before the afternoon was over, three long limos pulled up outside his house, and half a dozen guys jumped out and beat the crap out of him. You didn't mess with a nice Italian girl in Little Italy, Rochester, New York.

It was also a place where, when the warm weather came, the elders would take to their stoops and porches to gossip, share *vino*, and eyeball the kids playing baseball out front. Ours was a neighborhood that lived and died for playing ball. Back then, we didn't know much from drugs, pimps, or muggings. Back then, the closest we got to a gang was Mike Anachino's streetball team. All I wanted in life was for Anachino to ask me to play on his side. One nod of his head, and on the streets of Little Italy—you *belonged*.

Of course, I was dreaming.

You see, there were two small obstacles. One, I was as Irish as County Cork, freckles and all. In fact, my brother, sister, and I were the only Irish Americans in a ten-block radius. Strike two? Oh, yeah. I couldn't play ball.

Helen, my mom, knew exactly what was going on, and she didn't see any problem. She was waiting for me and my kid sister, Laura, as we dragged in from school one day. There she was, decked out in jeans and sneakers, her brown hair pulled back like she was twelve, grinning so hard the wrinkles around her eyes showed.

"I have something for you," she said, and from behind her back she produced two glaring red, white, and blue baseball gloves. They were the ugliest things I'd ever seen.

I looked at Laura. She looked at me. "Mom," we wailed in chorus.

"What's the matter? I'm gonna teach you to play. That's what you want, don't you? You wanna play ball with the other guys?"

"Everyone else's got brown gloves," I whined. "They'll laugh at us."

Mom's face took on a fighting expression I recognized: lips pursed, neck thrust forward like a chicken's. It was the same stubborn set I saw every time she dragged me over to a neighbor's house to ream out the mother of whoever had bloodied my nose that day.

"You kids don't listen, do you? I'm gonna tell you one more time. Never be afraid of what you look like to others. You miss out on a lot of fun that way." Mom's brown eyes were burning a hole through us now. "So I couldn't afford the leather gloves. That's not gonna stop us from playing ball. We're gonna give it our best, and forget about what other people might say. You don't want to miss out on something you might like, do you?"

Our Mom had a way of making the kind of sense you didn't argue with. So Laura and I followed her out to the backyard for our first lessons.

Mom played lousy. She threw the ball like a girl, from the elbow. Laura and I spent a lot of time ducking her wild pitches, sometimes not fast enough. But then, bruises were badges in our neighborhood.

I still laugh when I picture my mom in a catcher's squat. She'd hunker down like the world was coming to an end, pound her fist into her mitt, and yell at me to "throw one in here." But it was her return throws, arms flailing every which way, that were the challenge. Laura and I could catch anything after diving for Mom's balls.

And she kept us at it. It didn't matter how busy she was, several times a week she made sure we were in the backyard for a game. "Good one!" was her constant call—even if the "good one" had just bounced off her shin or over the fence.

Guess what? Laura and I got good, real good. In fact, before that summer was over, Laura was smoking at bat, smacking homers all the time. I thought my kid sister was as hot as any of the guys.

Mom's next move was to take Laura and me out to the street and make us play at the end of the block, in plain view of all the avid baseball critics lounging on their front stoops. At first they barely noticed, but after a while I saw them watching us, commenting and nodding, and I knew they liked what they saw.

But nothing from Anachino.

That didn't stop Mom. The following spring she had another surprise. "When you got talent, you gotta use it. I got something else for you." This time I knew it had to be something good—the packages were all gussied up in shiny red paper and ribbons. Laura and I attacked the wrappings and opened our boxes.

I'll never forget my sister's awed "Ohhhhh," or the new leather smell of those pigskin gloves. "And by the way, I've signed you up for Little League," Mom announced as an afterthought.

So now, every practice—Mom wouldn't let us miss one—the three of us would pile into our old Woodie and lurch across town to Russell Field. There she'd find a spot near the dugout and settle in for the afternoon to cheer us on.

That was a feat in itself, when I think about it. Russell Field was laid out on top of a landfill, and when the ninety sweltering degrees of New York humidity hit that underground mountain of decomposing garbage, the result was a spongy, weed-ridden, barf-inducing disaster. Our playing field was routinely voted the smelliest place in the universe. Of course, we kids hardly noticed. We were playing ball bigtime.

Then there were the evening games. Mom had this little problem with night blindness that nixed the Woodie after dark. But somehow she was able to coax and bargain rides out of the same moms with whom she used to have screaming matches. Helen always got us out to the ball game somehow.

School was out again. The boys of summer filled stadiums and streets. On my block I tossed the ball and watched Mike Anachino face down his rival as they both picked who was to be on *their* team.

And then it happened.

"Hey, Irish, you wanna play?" It was Anachino, and he'd just invited me to enter baseball heaven. If I lived to be a hundred, life couldn't get any better than this. I saw my little sister's face pucker. She smiled bravely before turning away, shoulders slumped. What was the matter with her? She knew as well I did that girls never, never got to play with the guys. And after all, Anachino wanted *me*.

I thought of Mom and how she didn't care what people thought, and of the two years Laura and I commiserated with each other over scraped knees and black eyes, walked past the Italians with our heads up, all sweaty and dirty after a game at Russell Field. How we talked proud about the ones we'd hit and tried to figure out those we'd missed. We'd gotten real tight playing ball together, me and Laura.

"You coming?" Anachino demanded.

Again I heard Mom's words. "Forget about what other people say, remember what's important."

"Nah!" I tossed the ball to Laura and she nabbed it with one hand. "Let's go, Sis."

"All right, okay, she can come too. She ain't so bad." This was more than a miracle. Anachino had just asked a *girl* to play street-ball. Laura and I stood grinning at each other like a couple of idiots.

"You coming or not?" Anachino was his usual self, but what did we care? We *belonged*.

→→→• ←←←

Mike says he didn't really appreciate his mom until he got older, but now he realizes that she was teaching him more than ball—she was teaching him what life was all about. He practices Helen Hayes' teachings in all aspects of his life, including his work. He takes time and care with his clients and always speaks the truth, even if it might mean losing a commission. And Laura? She's still on the field, proudly teaching baseball to children in Windsor, Colorado.

Reds' Excellent Adventure

From Michael Corr, 46, executive, hospitality industry

⫷⫷⫷⫷⫷

ONE DAY IN 1993, MY MOM, DOT, AT HOME IN NEW JERSEY, received a call from my dad, Reds, who was off visiting a horse show in Maryland.

"Hi, honey. Just wanted to tell you I'll be on the road for a week. I'm driving a team of Belgian draft horses across the country." Mom wasn't a bit surprised. But to understand why, we'll have to pull in the reins and back up a bit.

Francis "Reds" Corr is a hard-living man with the map of his mother's native Ireland stamped on his face. The fiery hair that inspired his nickname is long gone, but even today at seventy-nine, Dad stands six feet one, almost 200 pounds. He's got a sense of humor that won't stop, and a tenor so sweet he can bring tears to your eyes when he launches into a ballad. He'll fire up "Danny Boy" at anyone's request—anywhere, anytime.

Reds is retired now. He used to be a lineman for the Atlantic City Electric Company. Like most men of his generation, he is a

34

World War II veteran. But unlike most, he has not succumbed to backaches, sideaches, headaches. The man takes not one lick of prescription medicine. Neither does my mom.

They still live in the same house where I grew up, on a little barrier island off the coast of New Jersey, a hundred yards or so from the ocean.

Regular people, that's what they are. Good, regular people. Except for maybe in a couple of ways. For one, Dad was born one hundred years too late. He's a pioneer at heart—dreamed of wide open prairies, rolling hills of grass that ended in snow-topped mountains. He was convinced that the best of the American spirit lived and could be found in the West.

And the second irregularity? Most men of Dad's generation retire to putter around the house, take the wife to dinner, play a few links on the golf course. But Dad has always had a passion that's as Irish as his heritage—horses.

Reds was the oldest of five boys. His father died when he was fourteen. He got a job as a huckster, selling fruits and vegetables on the streets of Philadelphia from the back of a cart pulled by a horse named Peaches. I grew up on stories about Peaches.

"Do you know that your Uncle Joe, driving the old Ford, clocked Peaches and me going forty miles an hour over the Strawberry Mansion Bridge?"

"He did?" We'd listen wide-eyed, although we'd heard the story countless times.

"Yep. Forty miles an hour. That Peaches was some horse."

I guess she was. Forty miles an hour? Hell, I believe it. Reds was crazy enough to do it. He claims that after the war, the first place he went was to find Peaches, but the horse had died while he was overseas.

Over the years Dad's interest in horses waned a little. He'd go to the track on occasion, bet a few bucks here and there, do a little handicapping, but that was it.

Then, in 1983, he found out about a course at Cornell University teaching the use of draft horses for logging. Dad always had a particular interest in these massive work horses, so he signed up, showed up, and they were flabbergasted when they found out how old he was. He ended up being the star pupil, and everybody fell in love with him, but they didn't want to accept the liability of a man of sixty-six getting stepped on or hurt by those huge animals. When he applied for the course the following year, they said, "Jeez, Reds, thanks but no thanks."

Well, that was the end of that, we thought. In fact, we teased Dad. He loves beer, and we used to say it wasn't the horses he liked so much, it was the beer wagons they pulled.

But Dad's love for these animals didn't die. It smoldered along for ten years until he found out about a guy named Dick Sparrow, who had a ranch in Iowa and raised Clydesdales and Belgian draft horses.

Dick was planning to teach a course in Temecula, California, on how to drive two-hitch, four-hitch, and six-hitch teams.

Dad called immediately, only to find the class was full, but that Dick was going to be in Maryland for a horse show. Dad was told he was welcome to come visit.

Reds was absolutely thrilled. He went to Wilmington, Delaware, and stayed with my sister on Saturday night. To hear her tell it, he was up at the crack of dawn, driving her crazy. She felt pretty funny about the whole thing—thought Dad would just get in everybody's way, and he'd be home by noon at the latest. But she was dead wrong.

That day, Dad met Dick, a giant of a man himself, and no young-ster: six foot five inches, 240 pounds, in his early sixties. He and my dad hit it off famously. So much so that Dick invited Dad to assist him with the school in Temecula for two days, with part of the deal being to drive a team of Belgian draft horses across the country in a truck.

So here was my seventy-seven-year-old father calling my mother to tell her, "Honey, I'm driving some horses across the country. See you in a week."

→→→• ←←←

Dad went to Dick's ranch in Des Moines and helped him load eight 2,000-pound Belgian draft horses—the Coors Light show team with their fancy harnesses and huge wagon. Then off they went.

Dad didn't have the license to drive the truck, so his job was to take care of the horses—walk them, feed them, groom them. They stayed at the ranches of Dick's friends as they made their way to California.

Dad loved every minute of the trip. He woke up each morning happy to go to work, and fell asleep elated. The West was just as Reds had always imagined—the grassy prairies, the big sky, the colors of the dawn and sunset. I have a vision of him walking out on the prairie every night, a little John Wayne swagger in his step, marveling at how bright the stars could really be.

Everyone they met on the way embodied Dad's vision of the people of America—good, hardworking people who liked to have fun, didn't sweat the small stuff, and lived simply. They didn't care how old Dad was. They took him to heart for who he was.

By the time Dick and Reds reached the Stockton Fair in California, Dad was indispensable. So Mom got another call.

"Honey, it'll be another week—maybe more."

For ten days, he and Dick and the other hard-bitten characters at the fair slept in the barn with the horses. Just threw blankets down in the straw. Every night, they'd have "cocktails" while they played cards.

During one session, Dick set down his cards and rubbed his cheek. "Damned tooth's been killing me."

"So do something about it and quit complaining," said one of the wranglers.

Dick eyed the man for a minute, gulped down some whiskey and grabbed a set of channel locks. "Good idea."

The pliers disappeared into his mouth. One yank, a twist, and the tooth was dangling from the locks. Dick rolled his tongue around his mouth, felt the hole, and took another swig of whiskey. "Yep. That's better. Dealer's choice, boys? Five card stud."

Dad loved it. I think his stroll on the prairie was a little longer that night. He knew age wasn't important to these guys. And, apparently, neither were dentists.

From Stockton they headed south to Temecula for another ten-day course. Mom was expecting Dad's call.

"Honey . . ."

"I know, just another week," she laughed.

According to Dad, by this time he was helping to teach the course. This could be the story where the twelve-inch fish has somehow become three feet long, but I do know the guy's got a knack with these horses, so I wouldn't doubt it.

He celebrated his seventy-eighth birthday in Lodi, California, with Dick and eight Belgian draft horses. His seven-day trip had turned into a five-week adventure. When he finally came home to Mom, waiting patiently on her little island, he couldn't have been happier. It was like an infusion of energy for Reds, and we never grow tired of his stories about his days as a "teamster."

→→→ • ←←←

Mom has the same zest as Dad. They're independent souls with a great capacity for life. The trickle-down effect of their spirit is tremendous.

I'm forty-six, and a competitive athlete still. My sport is triathlon. Sometimes, I hear footsteps, and I think, *It's catching up to me.*

Then I think of Dad and his excellent adventure. He was willing to grab his opportunities, and enjoy them to the fullest. His energy has infused our whole family. We know that while we are living, we are *alive*. Even my kids think Gramps is the greatest thing since brown sugar.

→→→ • ←←←

In July 1995, Reds and Dot went out to Milwaukee for the Independence Day parade, which featured his buddy Dick driving a forty-horse team. Dick is one of the few people in the United States who can manage this feat. Reds and Dick swigged a few beers and told a few stories—just like old times.

Market Days

From Elizabeth Baumann, 70s, registered dietitian

$\mathcal{T}$HE SEATTLE OF MY CHILDHOOD WAS A BURGEONING CITY cut out of the wilderness of the Olympic mountains—not too many decades removed from its logging town origins. A dynamic town— singing the accents of Scandinavian lumberjacks, Cockney long- shoremen, and patrician academics holding court at the university.

There were two constants in my childhood. The first was my sea-captain father, who infused our home with all the allure of foreign climes and ports unknown. He was a storyteller of rare skill, and a vital presence even in his prolonged absences.

The second constant was my mother, Kathleen. We thought she was an Irish beauty with her large blue eyes and smartly styled dark brown hair. Mom was our stable force, a single mother in all but name. She was the well of things comfortable and un- comfortable, especially when we had been up to no good. How she always knew when we had been devils was beyond me, but it was also a secret source of pride. Mom was nobody's fool.

In those days children's lives were not structured every minute with soccer, gymnastics, ballet, or hours of homework. For us kids life revolved around Mom. And she was always there. Except on market days: those special days when Mom would venture on the trolley—she refused to learn to drive—to Pike Street Market.

The old Pike Street Market stood on a high bluff overlooking Puget Sound. Docked below were ships from the world over. Sprawling stalls stretched endlessly, overflowing with salmon, giant king crabs, crusty breads, foreign fruits and vegetables— items of which our local grocer could only dream. The excited accents of the Italian and Japanese merchants as they haggled with their customers added to the alien allure of this exotic place.

But for us Mom's trip to the market meant we'd arrive home from school to find the house empty. When we digested the fact that she was gone, a general shadow settled like a dark cloud, and we would drift away in an unvarying pattern.

Mary, the oldest, took herself off to the kitchen to solemnly perform her one known culinary skill—concocting tapioca pudding. I stood in awe of her. John hied himself upstairs and buried himself in a book. That left Joe and me.

Joe was my soulmate. If we could go outside rather than stay cooped up in the house, then by God, out we'd go, even if it was drizzling, as it usually was. This was Seattle, after all, and drizzle was our sunshine. So Joe and I would go to meet Mom, racing to the corner of Phinney and North 60th to await the arrival of the No. 21 trolley.

First we'd argue—should we stand by Woodland Park, or stay put on 60th? Woodland Park was a stop farther away from home, which meant we'd have to help carry the groceries longer, but it was a kid's paradise with the zoo and the playgrounds. Such a momentous decision made for a lively discussion. After Joe and I reached a truce, we'd gird our loins for the endless waiting for Mom.

Trolley after trolley passed. No Mom.

Darkness fell. No Mom.

Our next argument would be about how much longer to wait. That spawned another contentious debate. But never once did we leave our designated post.

Finally, the glorious moment arrived. On the exit platform loomed the unmistakable, pleasingly padded outline of Mom. As she descended, the drizzly, gloomy twilight was suddenly as shiny bright as the sun that bounced off the snow on Mount Rainier.

She was home.

Joe and I sprinted ahead with the shopping bags. As Mom came through the front door, the house seemed to glow like a saffron candle. I knew light couldn't emanate from a person like it did from a bulb, but Mom lit up the room just the same.

When she began to unload, it was a signal. An instant feast was in store, such a meal only to be enjoyed on market days. Laughter echoed through the kitchen—a place of silence until Mom came home.

Like magic, the best white linen was whisked onto the table. Out of the sacks, better than Aladdin's hoard, came the kippered salmon—rich and oozing with oil—and loaves of fresh French bread fragrant with yeast. Sometimes she'd bring home clams or Olympic oysters from Hood's Canal and we'd drink the cooking broth.

Then Mom would brew Mannings' coffee, the only time we were allowed such a treat. Oh, the rich, mouth-watering aroma. It filled the kitchen and spilled through the house. Butter, raspberry jam, Van de Kamp's cinnamon buns and maple bars, Mary's tapioca pudding, and home-canned peaches and pears from the cellar. I can still smell it and taste it.

We lost Mom when I was in my twenties, and Joe died a young man. I'd give anything to be able to wait once more with my brother for the No. 21 trolley—and Mom.

→→→• ←←←

Elizabeth carried on the tradition of small happinesses with her children: impromptu day trips to Mount Vernon; once-a-summer feasts of strawberry shortcake instead of dinner; August Tuesdays for swimming and picnicking on the Chesapeake Bay. She never knew if her kids appreciated it until she heard them tell their adventures to their children and she watched her mother's rituals played out in endless variations among her grandchildren. She marvels at how the tiny jewels of gladness are passed down through the generations, and hopes it never ends.

Life with Vava

By Brian Christopher Baumann, 15

My GREAT DREAM AS A YOUNG BOY WAS TO OWN A DOG. Just as Midas couldn't imagine that his power to transform all he touched into gold might be tinged with disappointment, I refused to consider that my longing could ever go awry. With my faithful canine companion by my side, I had no doubts that I'd become Superman, Batman, and He-Man put together. Yes! Lassie come home . . . to me.

But for years my path to ecstasy was blocked by an unyielding colossus known as my old man. Dogs, he proclaimed, were drooling, worthless "eating machines" only good for spreading fleas, worms, and hair. He often spoke approvingly of the fondness for canine exhibited by practitioners of certain Asian culinary traditions.

Perhaps his distaste for dogs grew out of his experiences as a mailman. He liked to regale our family with heroic tales of his exploits defending himself from attack by vicious brutes. His weapon of choice: a rolled up copy of the *Ladies Home Journal*. No dog alive, no matter how huge, vicious, or stupid, could weather a well-placed blow from the *Ladies Home Journal.*

So imagine my astonishment when I caught my old man sneaking a tiny, black Labrador puppy into the basement one snowy evening before my seventh Christmas. "That's a dog!" I squeaked.

My old man jumped at the sound of my voice, and spun his massive frame toward me. "Quiet!" He thrust the puppy into my arms, and peeked up the stairs, listening, no doubt, for my mother's footsteps. "Brian, can you keep a secret?"

"Cross my heart and hope to die." I immediately knew the oath was inadequate. I groped for a fate worse than death so he would know I meant business. "Or—or clean the garage for Mom."

Admiration lit his eyes. "Brave boy. Now you can help me hide it until Christmas morning."

My old man explained that he had paid a king's ransom for this pedigreed pooch. After much research into family dogs, he'd settled on the black Lab for its intelligence and temperament. "If we must have a dog, we're going to have a good one."

Over the next couple of days, I marveled at his ability to hide that pup from everyone. One time, he coolly passed off the telltale whimpering emanating from the basement as the snoring of my visiting grandfather. Grandpa sighed and snorted right on cue, and a disaster was neatly averted.

On Christmas morning, my mother almost fainted from the shock of seeing a black puppy festooned with a huge, red ribbon sitting under the Christmas tree. But my happiness was complete. After years of wandering in a petless desert, I had reached the Promised Land. Praise the Lord! And pass the kibble.

The dog of my dreams was always called Skipper, and that was the name I lovingly bestowed on my pup that Christmas. *Skipper.*

Leaper of tall fences, defender of seven-year-old boys. *Skipper.* Best dog in the world. No, wait—in the *universe.*

But before I had a chance to tell the rest of the family, my two-year-old sister toddled up to my dream, hugged her, then fell on her bum as the dog leapt on her chest. "Vava," she lisped between squeals of giggles.

"Our baby girl has named her," Mom cried proudly. "Vava."

Vava? No! How could anyone saddle that poor animal with the unrefined moniker of *Vava?* Jeez. The entire family cooed and chirped "Vava" all that long Christmas day, while I valiantly tried to insert "Skipper" into the conversation, to no avail. Oh, well, I could live with Vava. It was the presence of the dog herself that mattered, not what we called her. Right? Little did I know trouble was brewing in Paradise. This first frustration was just ominous foreshadowing.

My petite pup burgeoned overnight into the largest, mightiest canine I had ever seen. The dog's overwhelming strength surpassed my ability to control the beast, and I had to relinquish my duty of walking her to my old man.

He pitted his 250 pounds of muscle against Vava in a daily clash of titans. The family would hear half-audible curses when Vava's leash was produced, and wholehearted bellows as the dog towed him along while joyously doing her business in bucket-size loads.

Poor Mom, returning from endless obedience classes with the dog, looked as if she'd run the gauntlet, and Vava was not a whit better at obeying any of us. "Praise and love," Mom would chant. "That's what Vava needs. A lot of praise and love." I knew what she was really thinking: "Where's the *Ladies Home Journal*?"

Vava possessed a special talent for chewing on forbidden fruit. She gnawed her way out of her wooden puppy crate, and snacked on Mom's shoes and boots. The legs of the kitchen table held a certain piquant flavor that Vava found irresistible.

The dog was finally drummed out of the house and staked to a large pillar supporting our wooden patio, which was soon known, with good reason, as the "poop deck." This led to a new and terrifying trick. Vava found her howling voice. Morning, noon, night. Ahwoooo! Ahwoooo! Bark, bark, bark. *Ahwoooo!*

Neighbors began to leave death threats in our mailbox. The phone would ring during sleepless, early-morning hours, expletives spewing forth. I saw my old man wistfully eyeing a rifle in a nearby hunting store.

It didn't help any that my dog-loving Aunt Val was more than free with her long-distance criticism over our "mishandling" of the poor animal. "There are no bad dogs, only bad owners."

My old man sensed an opportunity to put Val's dog-handling skills to the ultimate test while ridding us of 120 pounds of pure trouble. "We're shipping Vava to Wisconsin. Let your Aunt Val take care of the damned animal."

To my family's eternal credit, we had tolerated Vava for a full six months. A hysterical Aunt Val, her house all but destroyed, lasted a mere two days before shipping the dog to a professional trainer.

Within a week the new owner's license to operate a kennel was threatened after Vava escaped from her enclosure and practiced her notable hole-digging skills on the velvet grass of the eighteenth green of a nearby golf course. Vava, the devil dog, was hastily banished to an understanding friend with a five-thousand-acre ranch in the great North Woods.

"The bears and coyotes better watch out," my old man prophesied. "They won't last a second with that dog."

But on certain cold, clear nights, we swear we can hear her howling at the moon. And every one of us, and probably the neighbors too, are seized with shivers of dread.

➤➤➤ • ◄◄◄

Once Brian's family recovered from the adventure of Vava, they discovered their true calling as cat people. For the last seven years they have shared their home with Baby, Frisky, Tigger, and six-toed Puma. No, they don't fetch. No, they don't sit, play dead, or roll over on command. And, yes, Brian's old man barely tolerates them. But they do give lots of love, and the family no longer receives death threats from the neighbors!

Extraordinary Gifts

*One joy scatters a
thousand griefs.*

—Chinese proverb

The Healing

From Beth Barkley, 50, systems analyst

✦✦✦✦✦

ℐ LIKED GAYLE ARRINGTON THE MOMENT I MET HER. ALMOST.

"Anybody home?" The call carried strong and clear into my backyard, eliciting a chorus of demented barking from my two German shepherds.

Who the hell is that? I was in the middle of a cleanup of multiplying piles of doggy-doo melting under the warmth of an unseasonably hot December sun, so I wasn't in the greatest mood.

"Hello, Beth? Beth Barkley?"

I straightened from my odiferous duty to see a heavy-set woman, her thin brown hair caught in a ponytail, squinting in my direction over John Lennon spectacles.

"Gayle Arrington," she offered. "White German Shepherd Club newsletter? We have an interview," she added at my blank stare.

I looked at her with undisguised irritation. She was early. "Unhook the gate, don't let the dogs out, and watch your feet," I yelled back.

My visitor followed my directions and carefully picked her way across my normally green and grassy verge. I began a lame explanation. "It was dark when I got back last night. My house-sitter—"

"If you've got another pooper-scooper," she suggested, "we can tackle this job in half the time." As I said, I liked Gayle Arrington right away.

→→→•←←←

Our interview that afternoon stretched into dinner at the local Thai restaurant. Panda, one of my dogs, and I were part of the USA's search-and-rescue contingent sent to Armenia in the aftermath of that country's devastating earthquake, and Gayle wanted every detail.

Our time together was the beginning of more than friendship. Gayle and I soon called ourselves "dog-in-laws." It was our way of feeling like family since neither of us had children, husbands, or living parents. Now when I was called for a search, it was Gayle who insisted on dog-sitting.

By 1990 both my shepherds were getting too old for the rigors of search work. Sharon Mann out of Winnipeg, Canada, breeds the finest search dogs in the world, so I considered myself very lucky when she called with the magic words, "I have a girl pup for you."

The following Thursday Gayle came with toothbrush and two new dog toys. Panda and Sirius parked their big bodies on either side of her chair, and rested their heads on her feet as we shared a good-bye bottle of Chardonnay. I wanted to bandy about names for the expected arrival, but my friend, who has no trouble talking a mile a minute, was unusually quiet. "Something wrong?" I asked.

"I've been feeling dragged out lately," replied Gayle. "Figured I might as well get a checkup. Probably just putting in too much overtime."

"Can you take some time off?"

"I'm thinking about it."

The sing-song chime of the telephone interrupted my next question. "Hold on a sec," I said, as I got up to answer.

It was Sharon Mann, the breeder. "I've got bad news," she began. Her Canadian brogue was clipped, too fast. "I took your pup to the vet for her health certificate and he detected a heart murmur." Sharon hesitated, and her next words came out slow, sad, apologetic. "He says she'll be lucky to see a first birthday. I'm so sorry, Beth."

"What's the matter?" Gayle mouthed.

I put my hand over the receiver. "The pup's very sick."

Gayle's broad face creased into concern.

"Beth?" Sharon asked.

"Yes, I'm still here."

"I'm glad I caught you before you left to come up here."

"Yes, I suppose it won't be any good coming up now."

"Wait a minute," Gayle interjected. "Your ticket's nonrefundable, Beth. Why don't you go anyway?"

I wasn't sure, still digesting the disappointment.

Gayle shooshed Panda and Sirius away, got up, and took the phone. "Hello, Sharon? I'm Beth's friend Gayle. She's coming anyway."

The next morning saw me in coach class to Canada.

→→➤➤ • ◂◂←←

Sharon's ranch-style home was exactly as I imagined: large, messy rooms overfilled with deep-cushioned sofas, most occupied by a contentedly snoring canine. It was an obstacle course of a house, scattered with chew toys, water bowls, and other animal-friendly paraphernalia. It reminded me of my own place.

The breeder led me to the kitchen, where a pup was curled up in the middle of a red plaid doggy cushion. Her fluffy white body looked small and vulnerable in the middle of all that color. Amber eyes met mine as I squatted beside her. She struggled to feet unsteady with sleep and nudged a cold nose into my outstretched fingers.

"Pick her up," Sharon instructed, and looked away as the pup smothered my face with wet swipes of her tongue. Now I could hear the painfully loud thump of an irregular heartbeat against my cheek. "She's a sweet thing, but no good for what you want."

Sharon was a decent human being, but breeding dogs was her living. The pup wouldn't be ill treated, but then it wouldn't get much attention either while it lived. The golden eyes that reminded me so much of my own Sirius melted into pure puppy love.

"I'd like to take her," I said. "I've got lots of room, she wouldn't be in the way, and perhaps your next litter …"

"You don't have to take her for that. I'll call you again when I think I have the right dog."

I carefully lowered Syrie Two—I'd already named her—into her bed and stood up. "That's not the reason." The truth was I didn't know why I wanted to take the sick pup home. How could I explain that it just felt like the right thing to do?

Sharon looked me up and down as if she were assessing me for breeding stock. "Follow me."

She strode ahead down a short hallway and opened a door. The room was lined with bookcases, filled with old titles long forgotten. The late afternoon sun streamed across pinewood floors with fond, slanting rays. Not a piece of furniture decorated the space. Only a five-foot-square wire dog pen dominated the center. Three barking canines immediately rushed their fence.

Two of them were your normal, white, German shepherd puppies, around ten pounds, noisy and curious. The third looked like it had taken up most of its mother's womb. I thought immediately of the enormous running back nicknamed "the Refrigerator." The dog even acted like the football player, lumbering up behind his siblings, shouldering them aside as if they were so many bubbles.

"Guess which one's the boy?" Sharon said.

"That would be too easy."

"He's called Czar. Czar the Terrible, actually. He's promised to the Winnipeg Police Department."

"Seems like a good place for him."

We watched the roly-poly tumbling of the pups in companionable silence. "I think you should take him," Sharon said.

"But—"

"Hear me out. Czar's a handful, yes. Rambunctious, hard to control. But with the right person, he'd make a damn good search dog. You're a pro, Beth. Take him, he'll be a good dog for you."

"But the Winnipeg police?"

Sharon grinned. "They'll wait for my next litter."

→→→•←←←

So the next day I was lugging two puppies home instead of one. Syrie Two went in the cabin with me. Czar the Terrible flew in baggage. I had no fear anything would happen to that gargantuan.

Gayle was waiting with two freshly groomed adult dogs and her famous lamb stew. As usual, she had to know every minute of my time away. I sat opposite my dog-in-law, with Syrie on my lap.

Gayle couldn't keep her eyes off the pup, only half-listening to my story. "May I hold her?" she asked suddenly.

"Of course."

"Pretty bad heart murmur," Gayle observed, nuzzling the dog against her cheek exactly as I had.

"The vet said she won't last the year," I told her.

"Well, that makes two of us."

"That's not funny, Gayle."

My friend put the white fluff ball on her lap and looked straight at me. "The doc called me with the results of my tests. I've got uterine cancer, Beth. Bad. I have about a year at most."

She continued to scratch the pup behind the ears. For her part, if Syrie Two was a cat she would have purred. Instead she pushed with all her puny might against the gentle pressure of Gayle's fingers.

"Beth, let me keep this one. You're gonna have your hands full with that monster you've brought home. I need something to take care of. Syrie and I can comfort each other."

I say stupid things when I'm in shock. "The vet bills will kill you, Gayle."

"It seems I'm dying already. Remember?"

"I'm sorry, I didn't mean . . ."

"I know you didn't, but *I* mean it. Let me have this pup."

"You can have anything I've got."

My friend's smile would have lit up the Astrodome. "Be careful what you offer," she teased.

I called Gayle every day until she told me to stop acting like a mother hen. "Syrie's so funny," she'd say, neatly changing the subject, then spend the next half hour relating how Syrie had kept her up half the night wanting to play before going to sleep on her belly. I didn't blame the pup. I often thought Gayle's belly would make a wonderful pillow. My dog-in-law never mentioned the weekly vet visits; the fear when Syrie's heart almost gave out; the expensive medication. And it took me a while to realize how skillfully she steered our conversation away from her cancer.

The next few months ran away for my dogs and for me. For Gayle and Syrie, too, so it seemed. My friend gave up her job as a customs inspector, and she and the pup took to visiting children's hospitals and senior citizens. Gayle told me Syrie was so popular that folks would buy her doggy treats and send letters to her. Their visits, Gayle often said, seemed to be the difference between living and living death for the people they touched.

I watched the year-mark approach and pass. Then it was eighteen months. How did a dying twosome manage to look so good?

Finally, the call came.

"Beth," my friend said, so quietly that I knew it was bad.

"Gayle—" I started to say.

A scream blasted my eardrum. "Beth, I'm in remission! Not a damn cancer cell anywhere. And I'm supposed to be dead, girl."

I felt a rush of such love, such relief. "And Syrie told me she ain't going anywhere, either. I mean, it's how long now?"

"One year, ten months," I mumbled. *And three days and eight hours,* I could have added.

I've never been much for destiny, fate, what have you, but I believe it was meant that I go to Canada, meant that I bring back a sick pup to a sick friend. It's one of the best things I've ever done in my life.

—→→►— • —◄←←—

Six years later, Gayle and Syrie Two are still going strong. They just moved to Florida, where they have a whole new group of people to bring cheer.

The Shared Loaf

From Anne Kerr, 60s, retired restaurateur

BEAUTIFUL SALONIKA, IN GREECE, WAS MY HOME, NESTLED by the crystal blue waters at the apex of the Gulf of Salonika. My sisters and I ran carefree through wide, shady streets, fragrant with flowering trees, olives, and almonds. The vermilions, fuchsias, and saffrons of the gardens were so bright my eyes ached with their beauty. Laughter was the music of my girlhood.

But in 1941 laughter died. I was ten years old. The Germans bombed my city for what seemed an eternity. They destroyed the port, the railroad, the airport. Whole blocks of homes tumbled into rubble, killing thousands, leaving more homeless.

April 2, 1941, is seared in my memory. My father was already fighting with the underground, so we were alone. I stood with my three sisters, clinging to my mother, as we watched the Nazis march through our streets. She squeezed my hand. "They have stolen your childhood," was all she said. On that day the vivid colors of my young existence darkened into a battle for survival.

We were beaten from our home. My mother watched the Germans burn it to the ground, and wept for irreplaceable heirlooms from countless generations. She was forced to trade our summer place for grain to feed us. An empty apartment became our shelter. We slept on the floor, grateful for at least a roof, subsisting on the little food or money our father and uncle managed to smuggle to us in the night.

On December 7, 1943, the Nazis came for the Jews. Men, women, children, it didn't matter, the German jackboots herded seventy-five thousand into oblivion. We were forced to line the streets and watch. Old folks were whipped to the ground with the butt ends of rifles because they could not walk fast enough. Children were kicked like soccer balls. Among them was my best friend, Renée. I never saw her again.

I remember my sister Maria as she rushed to say good-bye to our neighbor Dorina. As the two girls embraced and cried, a soldier raised his gun and smashed it against their heads. And for a moment, there was again a vivid color in my life—blood red.

Permeating it all was the hunger.

We were starving, despairing of our next meal. We never thought the day would come when all we would live for would be to see a new morning. Our time was spent scavenging for food. We learned to act fast, and together. On a rare occasion, a rumor would rush through the city like a brush fire—a butcher had meat, a baker flour.

It rarely rains in Greece, but on this October morning a cold drizzle fell steadily. The word came from a friend. A baker had bread.

It was my turn, so I grabbed my string bag and walked the ten blocks as fast as I could. When I got there, all I could see was an endless queue of spiritless people. I took my place, and waited.

Two hours passed. It was as if I hadn't moved. After three hours, I caught the smell. *Bread.* My empty stomach contracted, and I doubled over with the pain of it. Yet now I could look in the shop at the long, crusty loaves.

In front of me, a boy was pressed against the window, just as I was. His cheekbones cast deep shadows over the hollowed contours of his face. He seemed tall to me—a big boy of about fourteen or fifteen. His sleeves ended well above his wrists, exposing arms so thin I could have circled them with two of my fingers. He was starving.

The boy turned as if he sensed my stare. Our eyes met. For an instant I felt a kinship. They'd taken his childhood, too. We shuffled forward together.

We'd waited for four hours. Finally, we were inside. In the crush of people, I couldn't see the supply of bread anymore, but ahead of me the baker handed the gaunt boy his loaf. He turned. His brown eyes were enormous, alight. He had food.

The man scowled as I stepped up to the counter, "Bread's gone. I don't have anymore."

He couldn't mean to be cruel. "Please, sir," I managed.

"Sorry. No more."

A collective groan arose behind me, and people drifted away. The boy didn't move. He clutched his bread to his chest, a desperate look on his face. Then his expression softened and he smiled. I remember his smile, because it was so kind. Did I return it? I can't recall.

With a quick snap, he broke the precious loaf into two pieces. "Here, little girl, this is for you." In his hand he proffered half his bounty.

I couldn't believe it. I knew his belly ached as badly as mine. To allay the pain of starvation, even for a short time, was a greater treasure than all the riches of Olympus. This bread might be the difference between life and death.

"I want you to have it," he urged and thrust it into my hands.

My fingers brushed his and stayed for a moment. I suddenly realized how truly isolated we had all become one from another. I didn't want my new friend to go.

His thin shoulders lifted in a shrug. He smiled once more, then stepped quickly through the door into the rain.

"Thank you! Thank you!" I called.

I slid the bread into my bag and followed him. I hadn't even asked his name, or offered him my coins. The street in front of me was a mass of huddled gray figures. Where was he? I looked left and right, and thought I saw him turn a corner. I ran to it, but he was gone.

I never saw my friend again. But that boy restored my faith in people. In the bitter years to come, I had only to remember him to survive hell. His kindness was as nourishing to me as his gift of a shared loaf.

→→→ • ←←←

Anne came to America at the age of eighteen when she married Don, an Army Air Corps officer. But each year she returns to her beloved Greece. She has vowed never to forget the war years, and her stories keep the memories alive for her children and grandchildren.

We Believe in You

By Mary Pesaresi, 40, writer

FIVE YEARS AGO I BEGAN TO PURSUE A PASSION THAT HAD BEEN smoldering inside of me before the birth of my two daughters.

I needed to write.

The opportunity came when my younger girl started kindergarten, and my time was no longer devoted to the constant demands of preschool, meals, and diapers. I spent every spare moment at the typewriter, wrestling with characters who invaded my dreams, with plot twists I unraveled as gleefully as a puzzle master.

Before my marriage I had written and produced plays, but I had no idea of the business of book publishing. I belonged to no writers' groups, had no contacts, no acquaintances who were writing. I didn't even know correct manuscript mechanics, and I didn't dream the industry was as much about rejection as joy. In short, I was a babe in the woods, floundering along on sheer adrenaline and true love.

Months later, my rambling, nine-hundred-page, eighteenth-century historical novel sat proudly on my kitchen table. Suddenly, writing it wasn't enough. Now I wanted it read. Not just read, but exclaimed over, praised, admired, and loved. And I knew the one person who was generous enough, yet honest enough to trust with my baby. My sister-in-law, Trish.

"I've written a novel," I explained over the phone.

There was a pause, and an intake of breath. "My God," Trish murmured, her awe heady wine to my creative muse.

"Will you read it and tell me what you think?"

"A novel! Why didn't you tell me? Of course I will."

The next day I stood motionless before their door, almost afraid to knock. *What if it's awful? I shouldn't have come.*

The door flew open before I could turn away. Trish stood smiling at me—beautiful, as usual. Her model-slim figure and lovely face are what the ordinary observer sees. But the extraordinary observer, like my brother who fell in love with her, is struck by the kindness in her eyes, the sweetness of a smile that holds a knowledge of tragedy through loss without surrender to bitterness.

I wanted her to draw on her depth of character to tell me if what I had written was true. And I depended on her love to be gentle in critique.

Trish removed the manuscript from my hands as delicately as if it were written on diamonds. "I'll read it right away."

I waited, never more than three steps from the phone. Days slipped by. With each passing hour, my confidence faded. I could never be a writer. What arrogance in my soul let me believe such a fantasy? I wanted the ordeal finished, for good or ill. I dialed Trish's number.

My brother picked up the phone. "Hello?"

"Um, Jim, is Trish there?"

"No, Mare. She's shopping."

"Do you know if she's read my book?"

"Yeah. She read it. Look, Mary, let me have her call you."

My stomach was in knots. *Yeah. She read it.* I stared at my manuscript, and wanted to light a match to each page. Instead I spent the day scrubbing bathrooms until my brush was flattened, and the tile scored with scratches I'd regret later.

Life goes on, but dinner that evening was a silent affair.

The next morning, after seeing my husband off to work and driving the girls to school, I reviewed the day's duties—beds to make, piles of laundry to wash, errands to run, dinner to cook. The allure of spending the next few hours as a frivolous, bon-bon-eating couch potato seemed preferable to housework, and anything was better than vain ambition.

I was staring at my car keys, trying to figure out where one might find the nearest bon-bons, when I heard a knock on the front door. Bad timing. I was in no mood to deal with Jehovah's Witnesses this morning.

No Bible-toting folks ready to redeem my soul awaited me. Instead, Jim and Trish stood on the threshold, each hugging a large carton and balancing a smaller box on top.

"Where do you want it?" Jim asked in greeting.

"Huh?"

"Your computer. Where do you want it?"

"Huh?" So much for eloquence.

"If you're going to be a writer, Trish and I figured you'd need a computer. So where would you like it set up?" Jim smiled a crooked, charming grin, left over from his mischievous childhood. "Remember yesterday, when I told you Trish was shopping? She was buying this."

"It's because I love your book," Trish said simply.

"She told me you have talent. That's good enough for me," Jim added. "But you need a computer to really get going, so here it is."

How could my younger brother and his wife afford this? The business they had created was just beginning to pay off. This gift was too much, like Rockefeller endowing a university. But hey, Trish loved my book! My Lord, Trish loved my book. "I can't," I gasped.

"You bet you can," Jim said. "Trish and I figure someday one of your books will get published. It might not be this one. It might be your fourth. But it'll happen."

I had to laugh. "My fourth! I don't know if I'll have the stamina to last that long."

"You'll last," Trish stated. "There's too much love in your writing for you to quit. We believe in you."

I remember that happy day in detail. The Epson computer, its color monitor, keyboard, and thunderous dot-matrix printer, were the most wondrous of human creations. And Jim and my sister-of-the-heart Trish were perhaps the most generous people I might ever know.

It wasn't until months later I joined writers' groups, learned about publishing and the market, met editors and agents, and discovered that my monolith was completely unsalable.

I also discovered the sad truth about this profession I'd chosen. It's a lucky, talented, and select few who achieve the moniker of "published" every year. Rejection has to be viewed as a learning experience, not a personal indictment. No writer takes it for granted that his or her next project will find a home in the book-stores. And rejection hurts. Always.

Yet whenever I sit before Jim and Trish's computer and my fingers touch the keys, I remember that someone believed in me.

Their faith in me is the best healer of soul wounds, the best motivator to continue in the face of dismissal, and the greatest inspiration to make my writing as good as it can be.

Although the dedications in my books might not always mention Jim and Trish, I want them to know they are the heart and soul of every story I tell.

Jim and Trish weathered the storm of all ambitious entrepreneurs to see their business become a rousing success. Mary is as proud of their enterprise as they are of Mary's books.

Strength

God gave us burdens,
also shoulders.

—Yiddish proverb

Against All Odds

From Anne Rutherford, 38, office manager

My son Tommy was eleven years old when I remarried
and transferred with my new husband to a suburb of Washington,
D.C. It was a move of great hope and joy, but it was also terribly hard
for Tommy and me.

We hailed from rural Arkansas, where we had the comfort and
support of a large church-going family. Back home, Tommy was a
popular kid with a ton of friends. He was outgoing and friendly,
and loved both church and school activities. When we came to
D.C., it was big, confusing, exciting, and scary all at once. Tommy
was enrolled in a school that was huge compared to his old one,
and he didn't know a soul.

He had to cope with another problem. He is deaf in one ear,
and his hearing is limited in the other. In Arkansas, Tommy
handled it by sitting at the front of the classroom, where he could
read lips if he couldn't quite pick up the voices of his teachers. All
his instructors were aware of his disability and cooperated with
him. As for Tommy's friends, none of them gave it the slightest
thought.

I explained my son's condition to his new teachers in D.C. They seemed concerned, and pledged to help him. At first they did.

Unfortunately, the bright promise of my marriage did not last. It was only a few years before Tommy and I were on our own again, but this time without my family close by.

I know it's hard for an African-American teenage boy in our urban environments, and suddenly Tommy had no father figure in the house. But I didn't want to return to Arkansas. I'd found a good job with a great company, and I thought Tommy was in the right school. So once again I was mother, father, and breadwinner.

It was a struggle, but we made it a happy one because we had each other. I kept my son busy—school and extracurricular activities were part of his schedule—because I know what happens to kids when they lapse into idleness. Most boys I see in trouble have too much time on their hands. And I kept him immersed in our church. It's hard to go astray with the Lord to guide you.

Things were going well when Tommy started high school, and I was pleased we were such a team. Then it happened, so gradually it was barely discernible. Tommy began to withdraw. He'd come home and lock himself in his room. He used to share everything with me, but now, when I asked about his day, his answer was either "fine" or "okay." His warm, outgoing personality was snuffed out, and I didn't understand why.

At first I thought it was puberty. Kids go through a lot of emotional turmoil during that period, and it's not unusual to see such changes. But it alarmed me, and I wasn't going to wait around, hoping my son would tell me what the problem was.

The day I contacted Tommy's school to make an appointment with his principal was the same day I received the worst wake-up call of my life.

"This is Prince George's Hospital. Your son is in the emergency room. He's been hit by a truck."

The floor fell out from under me, and I broke all land speed records getting to that hospital. The pictures playing in my head were the worst torture I had ever undergone. When I finally rushed into the ER, the nurse assured me that Tommy had suffered cuts and bruises, and thank God, very little else.

For the first few minutes, all I could do was sit on the bed and hold him.

"It's okay, Mom. Don't cry," he said. "I'm fine."

Okay. Fine. I'd become sick of those words. "What happened?"

"Nothing."

I pulled a chair next to him and held his scratched and bandaged hand. "Tommy, you're going to tell me, or I'm going to sit here all night long asking you the same question over and over. What happened?"

"You got too much to worry about, Mom. I'm okay."

"What happened?"

My son pressed his lips together tightly and he tried to escape my stare. But every time he turned his head, I moved so he was forced to look me in the eyes. "You can tell me anything, Tommy."

Tears slipped over his cheeks when I said that. "They pushed me," he finally whispered, "in front of a truck."

I had to keep calm. "Who?"

"The kids at school. They hate me. Every day they beat me up or push me around. It's some older guys. I wouldn't help them when they wanted a lookout."

A lookout? I could only imagine what they needed a lookout for. My worst nightmares took shape as I stared at my battered and bruised boy. "Oh, Tommy. Why didn't you tell me before?"

"How could I, Mom? I didn't want them to hurt you. You're working so hard."

Like a dam bursting, everything poured out of Tommy. I listened in horrified silence to the taunts, the threats, his fears. "I'll do anything you need me to do," I said when he finally stopped. "We'll switch schools. These kids won't let up."

Tommy stared at the wall, saying nothing. Then very quietly, he said, "No, Mom, it don't work like that. Every school around us has gangs. I just gotta face it."

"We'll face it together," I told him. It was a vow.

I have never seen such an expression in any eyes as Tommy's when he smiled at me. "Then we'll be okay, Mom."

I saw a difference from the day Tommy returned to school. He went to each of his teachers in turn and demanded a seat in the front of their classes, and he got them.

That same day I called on the one instructor I felt could make a difference for my son on a daily basis. He was the head of the ROTC department, and he had previously expressed an interest in Tommy. I explained to him what had happened. This man took my boy under his wing as if he were his own.

Oh, our battles continued for quite some time. They didn't all of a sudden stop because we'd resolved to fight them. But gradually, Tommy's self-confidence grew, and under the protection of his ROTC commander, he blossomed.

My son and I took every step of the way through high school together. No, I didn't hover over him like some maternal guardian angel. But when troubles came, he knew he could turn to me.

Three years later Tommy was captain of the ROTC color guard. When I saw him take the field in his uniform and lead the marchers, I was overwhelmed with pride.

On the day of his graduation, Tommy handed me his diploma. "I couldn't have done this without you, Mom."

What will Tommy accomplish during the rest of his life? I can hardly wait to see. As mother and son, when we stand together, and draw on the other's strength, we can face anything the universe throws at us . . . and triumph.

→→→•◄◄◄

In August 1996, Anne and Tommy went back to Little Rock, Arkansas: Anne to marry a college sweetheart, and Tommy to audition for the choir of Philander Smith College, which sang for President Clinton at his inauguration.

Everyday Hero

From Betty Wall, 70s, homemaker

❧❧❧❧❧❧

I WAS DRIVING TO WORK ON THE MORNING OF NOVEMBER 30, 1947. The day was wind-whipped and rainy, with low hanging clouds that turned Puget Sound a choppy iron gray, and hid the snow-capped peaks framing my city of Seattle. There was a nip in the air that chilled straight to the bone, and I flipped on the radio for diversion. That's when I heard the news.

"This just in. A plane has crashed at Bow Lake Airport. Apparently, it slid off the runway, down a twenty-four-foot embankment, and plowed into a car on the Des Moines Highway where it intersects South 188th Street. The plane has burst into flames. I've just been told it's Alaska Airlines, in from Anchorage, a C54 with twenty-eight people on board."

The news made me shudder. I hated to fly. Bucking and heaving over the mountains into Seattle was my idea of hell. But I was a heedless twenty-something, and as with all young people, I saw things from a self-centered point of view. This crash didn't affect me. Maybe my brother Joe, who worked as a ticket agent at the airport, could give us some juicy details at the end of the day. But that was all.

76

"This reporter has been told that a bystander has rushed into the flaming plane, and emerged dragging a badly burned man."

That stopped me for a minute. Wow! What a hero. But heroism so shortly after World War II seemed commonplace. In my generation we never boasted about our accomplishments, never blew our own horn.

My veneer of sophistication was torn for only a brief instant before I settled into its comfortable skin again. "Wonder what he thinks is in it for him?" I remember muttering. "Maybe Hollywood will come calling."

When I arrived home that evening, I had frankly forgotten about the crash and the man who had rushed into the flames. My brothers and I were all living in the house of our childhood, as our mother had passed away suddenly. I had pulled up roots in California and come home to take care of the "baby" in the family, Bill, who at fourteen was a strapping six-footer.

The evening routine was always pretty much the same, unless I had a date. I cooked dinner for everyone and we usually could look forward to a rousing discussion at the table, led with caustic humor by my brothers Joe and John. But tonight, Joe was silent. When we asked about the crash, he simply shrugged.

"You'd think *you* were the guy who ran into that burning plane," John teased.

"I was," Joe said quietly, and left the table. We laughed.

Then the reporters started calling. Joe refused to talk to them, and we could barely register what had happened. We had a hero for a brother, but we halfway dismissed the enormity of the act when Joe himself wouldn't tell us anything. We went to bed in a state of disbelief.

The next morning, the *Seattle Times* ran a front-page story on my brother:

NORTHWEST AIRLINES AGENT
SAVES BURNED MAN

Fellow workmen told a story of heroism in connection with the Bow Lake tragedy yesterday, when a young Northwest Airlines passenger agent risked his life to enter the burning plane and pull a badly injured man out of the craft.

Reticent about telling of the act, the veteran of wartime service with the Army refused to give details of the rescue.

Another Northwest employee, Pete O'Brien, pointed Wall out as a hero. "Joe heard calls for help from within the plane," O'Brien said, "so he wrapped something around his head and crawled into the rear of the cabin. He came out dragging a man who was really badly burned but still alive. Joe was pretty woozy from the smoke."

"What did you wrap around your head?" Bill demanded.

"My suit jacket," Joe answered.

→→•←←

It wasn't until years later that Joe told me his story. "I could see, feel, a sense of horror, knowing these people, so near, yet so far away, were piteously begging for help. I couldn't live with myself if I had ignored them."

After he dragged the injured man from the plane, the guy clung to Joe. "Am I going to die?" he asked.

"Of course you're not," Joe said. My brother groped for the only comfort he could give under such bizarre circumstances. Joe, the

Jesuit-trained half-believer, baptized the man and recited the Act of Contrition. It gave the poor fellow peace, and he recited the prayer as he could. Joe sent his spiritual brother to heaven the best way he knew how. Later, the man's family wrote to Joe. "You have restored our faith in humanity," they said.

>>>>• •<<<<

None of us could oust this act from our thoughts with a cynical "What's in it for him?" The wondrous spirit of my brother had been challenged, and he rose to action, risking the holocaust to save a stranger. When rescue workers arrived at the crash site, they were able to save sixteen more passengers. The man Joe pulled from the wreck died of his injuries.

The world forgot Joe's heroism with a snap of its fingers. But I could never dismiss it. He was an inspiration to me. He never dreamed, until I told him decades later, that I lived on his example as a bulwark against the constant refrains of our self-centered, materialistic society: "Don't trust anyone." "Watch your back."

Joe was not a hazy figure in a black-and-white newspaper, nor a breathlessly interviewed "someone" flickering across my TV screen, then forgotten. This is how most people know those commonplace souls who flare with a courage that shows a pure, bountiful heart. I'm luckier. Joe was my brother. He was real.

>>>>• •<<<<

Joe's independent spirit served him througout his life as a businessman with offices in such far-flung places as Richmond, New Orleans, and Seattle. Although childless himself, Joe was the unchallenged favorite uncle with all of Betty's children.

Zebra Stripes

By Jennifer Shingleton, 15

$\leftleftarrows$

My PARENTS SAT ON THE BLUE AND WHITE CHECKERED couch with several old photo albums open on their laps. They looked through the miscellaneous pictures, and in each one a bright smile illuminated Mom's countenance. She has always been the type of person who smiles, even in her passport pictures.

My father, on the other hand, rarely smiles, not because he isn't happy, but because he is a serious man.

The two of them flipped to a picture of their fifteenth anniversary. My mother's wrinkle-free skin made her look young, especially with her glad, fulsome smile. My father's gray hair aged him, but he appeared particularly wise.

In the picture Mom was holding a glass of champagne, Dad a glass of water. Mom takes great delight in fine wines, but they give Dad migraines. We had to have two cakes for their anniversary. The rich chocolate mousse cake with hazelnuts was Mom's. Dad ate angel food—nut free, chocolate free.

I squeezed in between my parents on the couch as they picked up their wedding album. There they were, sitting in a flower-draped carriage. Mom, in her formal white gown, looked as if she belonged in the ballroom of a palace. My father was handsome in a sporty blue blazer, eminently suitable for watching a match by the grass courts of Wimbledon.

Mom's hat was tipped slightly on her head, and she cradled a beautiful bouquet of flowers. Her face was alight, as if the sun had directed a gentle beam encircling only her.

"I knew the minute I saw her," Dad said, tapping the picture with one fingertip.

"What nonsense," Mom laughed.

"No, really. The moment I saw you."

And I knew what was coming: the story of how they'd met. Dad was a senior in high school, top of his class, and a fierce competitor in sports. Mom was a freshman, very intelligent, but more laid back when it came to the occasional B on her report card. And sports to Mom were strictly fun.

"Tell me the story again, Dad."

"I ran out onto the basketball court, my teammates beside me, and I saw a beam of light shining on her face. I knew. Not a shadow of a doubt."

"I'm afraid I took a little longer," Mom laughed.

I glanced again at their wedding picture. Mom looked just like I imagined when Dad saw her in the crowd of spectators.

My father fished out another album, and we stopped to examine a print of a zebra. Its black and white stripes were intertwined perfectly. Against the lush green trees and fields, the contrast was sharp and hit you like a kick from behind.

This has always been my parents' favorite animal picture. Perhaps it is the eternal puzzle of whether the zebra is black with white stripes or white with black stripes that intrigues them. Both are certainly equal. Both are inseparable. It is impossible to completely solve or understand its pattern.

But I studied them, not the zebra, finding them every bit as fascinating, and wondering how their very different personalities, likes and dislikes, meshed so beautifully.

As if they had the same thought, my parents stopped looking at the pictures and began to talk about some financial business.

Mom sipped her mug of strong, black coffee, and stated her opinion on the matter. Dad drank his skim milk, settled his square-framed glasses on his Roman nose, and talked for five minutes in a wise, authoritative voice, proposing a different answer. Despite his efforts, my mother smiled, and interjected points for her side.

I left the room, unable to decide who had the better argument, but I knew they would come up with the right solution.

And the answer, as always, would be striped.

--->>-•-<<---

Jennifer is a gifted, serious student who takes after her father in academic pursuits and, like her mother, loves to travel. She is very concerned about her world community. Last summer, she and her older sister, Elizabeth, spent a month in Tibet with a missionary group helping to build a church.

I Remember Allison

By Shannon Elaine Denny, 23, writer

✿✿✿✿✿

$\mathcal{M}$Y MOTHER ONCE TOLD ME, "YOU WILL NEVER UNDERSTAND the depth of love a mother has until you have a child of your own." I suppose I took this to mean that once I had nourished my child and had the opportunity to watch it grow, I would understand this more fully. How was I to know Mom's wisdom would take on a whole new meaning, deeper than I would have ever thought I was capable of comprehending? But it did, and this is my story.

I married my high school sweetheart at the age of eighteen. Scott and I were desperately in love and settled down immediately into a stable life. My husband worked in a factory, and I was a waitress.

A few months after our wedding, we received a surprise. Our first son was to be born in December. It was my fairy tale come true, for I had always dreamed of having a family, and my husband and I prepared for our child with great anticipation.

Cory Scott arrived on a picture perfect winter's day, December 4, 1992. The trees were heavy with snow, and I held a beautiful miracle in my arms. Everything was still and perfect.

Eight months later I was pregnant again. This time my husband
I weren't sure we were ready for another baby. But our love for
children and our natural excitement conquered fear, and we
began to count the days, as we had with Cory.

Almost immediately, I knew I was going to have a little girl—
call it mother's intuition—and her name would be Allison Haley.
What a feminine name, I would think as I tried a hundred times to
picture her little face. I would imagine her daddy fixing her hair
with barrettes, only to give up and leave it in a tangled mess of
curls. It was a precious, secret fantasy that always made me smile.

In the third month of pregnancy, I heard my daughter's heartbeat. I was so moved I asked Scott to come to my prenatal appointment the following month so he could hear it for himself.
We had very little money, so we decided that listening to our
baby's life rhythm would be our anniversary gift to each other.

The awaited day came. We stepped into the doctor's office and I
lay on the table, holding my husband's hand, the two of us smiling foolishly. The doctor pressed the flat microphone against my
belly and I held my breath, straining to hear every beat, every
pump of that little heart. But there was nothing except static.

The doctor frowned, and tried another position. Again, nothing.
"Oh, well," she said cheerfully. "Looks like baby doesn't want to
cooperate today."

"Why can't we hear anything?" Scott asked.

"Baby's on its side," the doctor explained. "Why don't you come
back in a couple of days, and we'll see if baby's done a flip."

The doctor wasn't worried. Why should I be? I returned alone
two days later.

"I still can't hear anything," my doctor said, frowning.

"Should I be worried?"

A smile softened the taut lines across her forehead. "No use borrowing trouble. We'll just do an ultrasound and see what kind of funny position this child has managed to contort itself into. Simply routine."

My mother accompanied me to my ultrasound appointment. Mom and I were giggling over discovering the sex of my baby when the technician entered.

"Hello. This will feel cold," she said, and slapped what seemed to be frozen petroleum jelly all over my stomach.

"No kidding," I teased, but the woman didn't smile.

I refused to let her attitude affect my mood. I clung to humor as to a life raft. It seemed like hours as she took the baby's measurements and jotted notes. "I'll call the doctor with the results," she said, as she left the room.

Mom held my hand, and squeezed it. "Everything will be fine."

Neither of us said anything while we waited. Then the technician returned, beckoned me down the corridor, and silently pointed to a phone on her desk. "Your doctor's on the line," she said, before she left.

I picked up the phone. "So, is it a boy or a girl?"

"I'm so sorry. The ultrasound showed that your baby has died."

"No, doctor," I gasped. "You have me mixed up with someone else. This is Shannon. My baby's in a funny position, that's all." *Please, God. That has to be all.*

"I'm so terribly sorry."

"No!" I collapsed against my mother, trying to deny the cruel joke that I knew to be true, and wept for the child, lifeless and still in my womb.

I don't remember the ride to Scott's work, but I do remember the doctor describing to my husband and me our options. I could either check into the hospital today, and they could induce my labor, or I could wait until I felt emotionally ready.

What would I say now if somebody asked my due date? How could I get through telling them my child would forever be silent and never draw its first breath? The thought was so horrifying that all I wanted was to hide and end this nightmare. "Now," I said. "Immediately."

It took two days for the contractions to begin. I was in a room at the end of the hall of the labor and delivery ward. I heard the woman in the next room moaning in labor. Moments later, I heard her baby's cries. I died inside, positive I would lose my mind with grief.

About an hour later, my water broke and the baby slid into the birth canal. I screamed for a doctor to help me. My mother raced down the hall and begged a nurse to come. But there were too many women in delivery, and I was not a priority because this was not a live birth.

Seconds later, my baby was born. My husband and my mother tried to soothe me as the child lay there, so quiet on the table, still attached by its umbilical cord. It was finished—hours of labor without one moment of joy.

A few minutes later, my doctor arrived. "It's a girl," she said. Somewhere, in some far distance, I heard wailing and realized it was me. I saw my husband as he stared at our little, perfectly formed daughter, and knew that he, too, was mourning from the bottom of his soul.

I held my daughter, wrapped in a blanket of pink. Allison seemed to have no weight, but I could smell her scent—a mysterious essence of baby. "She smells just like a rose," I whispered to my mom. "Just like a rose."

I was released that day. The nurse gave me a tiny yellow dress by which to remember my sweet daughter. I slept with it for weeks before I was able to put it away. And to this day I thank God for my son, Cory. It was from his unconditional love, as always, that I drew my strength.

About a month later, my mother told me of a young woman who lived nearby. She had lost her daughter in her ninth month of pregnancy. My heart went out to her. I picked up the phone.

"Hello," I said. "I know you don't know me, but I understand what you are going through. I would like to buy you lunch and listen when you're ready to talk."

She thanked me quietly, and I could hear my own sadness reflected in her voice. A week later, she called. We went to lunch and she handed me a Polaroid picture that she had not shown to anyone. It was her daughter, minutes after her stillbirth. I put my arms around the woman and for that little time, it eased the pain that enveloped us both.

My friend calls me sometimes to ask me how she is going to face a baby shower or her daughter's birthday and I remember the platitudes of well-meaning friends that hurt so badly.

"You'll have other children."

"It's not like you knew her or anything."

"Something must have been wrong with the child."

So I am careful with my words and tell her what my heart believes. We will see our daughters again someday. We will live through this and be stronger, little by little.

Life teaches us hard truths, and God knows the stillbirth of Allison was the hardest I've ever had to face. But I have grown stronger, and I've learned a valuable lesson. I believe that we should reach down inside ourselves and help those people whose shoes we have shared. Maybe their feet are tired and we can carry them . . . if only a little way, if only a little while.

→→→• ←←←

Shannon and Scott had a healthy, green-eyed, brown-haired boy, Andrew, on November 1, 1994. The third and last child they plan to have is due in September 1996. Shannon knows it will be a daughter.

I'll Be There

From Dan Aufdem-Brinke, 23, student

THERE ARE CERTAIN MOMENTS IN LIFE THAT CHANGE YOU forever. One of mine came in my eleventh year.

I've lived on the outskirts of this little nothing town on the side of a mountain all my life. Our house hides off a dirt road, a quarter of a mile in from what Mom says is the back of nowhere. To get to our place is a major exercise in patience and maneuverability. If the ruts don't swallow your tires, the hill will pull you back down, or the ditch will take your rear as you squeeze 'round a corner. But as with all good things, it's worth the extra effort.

You see, it's beautiful here. I love the woods, the animals, the quiet, and our house that crowns the hill as if it grew from the forest itself. When I was little, my dad's parents lived down the drive from us. I'd stop by almost every afternoon, when the school bus dropped me off. Grandma always had hugs and treats for me and my kid brother, Jason.

Our cousin lived here, too. And we had the comfortable security of knowing Mom would be home when we trudged up the hill.

Mom's a writer, and her office is in the house. The solitude and beauty are perfect for her chosen profession. Mom described it as our own Walden enclave.

When I was eleven, things changed fast. Mom and Dad divorced. Grandma and Grandpa moved from our mountain to Florida. My cousin left for Hagerstown, not too far away, but it might as well have been the end of the world as far as I was concerned.

Suddenly, it was just Mom, me, and Jason. I didn't tell her— I didn't let on to anybody—but it felt like everyone had abandoned us.

It wasn't easy for my mom back then. She spent eight to twelve hours a day at the computer, and took care of her fan mail, but now there was no family around to help. Jason and I took out the trash and stuff, and Mom made sure we cleaned up our rooms to her satisfaction. But now there was only her to do the cooking and take care of us.

That winter brought the worst storms. We had snow piled up against the windows for, like, forever. Half the time our car couldn't get down the hill so we got stuck at home a lot. Mom made it fun with games, hikes in the woods, and storytelling. Then, I don't know why, I started to torment my kid brother.

Jason's three years younger than me, and I'd always pulled the firstborn superiority bit. But now my greatest mission in life seemed to be to aggravate him to death. I'd poke him in the ribs or pinch him hard until he cried, and that would upset Mom. One day I went too far.

We were in the bathroom together, and I picked up the hair-spray can, hit the button, and this sticky mist shot right into his eyes. His face screwed up, and he screamed and screamed. I was scared. I didn't mean to hurt him, it just happened. Mom was really mad at me that time.

It didn't help that I suddenly turned into a house wrecker. I'd walk through the living room or kitchen, and without thinking, I'd ball a fist and smash one of her ashtrays or vases. It was like I had no control over myself. I *had* to break something.

Mom has these neat plants in every room, and I love flowers. One day I remember seeing her prized African violets on the window sill. Suddenly, this irrational fury took over, and I ripped them apart. I couldn't even tell her why I did it, and I hated making her look sad.

"What's wrong, Dan?" she'd ask.

"Nothing."

"Don't you understand? I can't help you if you don't tell me what's wrong."

"I told you, Mom. Nothing's wrong."

So I'd be grounded again, and Mom would ride my tail even harder to keep me in line. And always she'd try to get me to open up. The funny thing was, I was glad she made me leave off Jason, finish my chores and my homework, and all the other stuff I was supposed to do. Only I couldn't let her see it.

At school things were going from bad to worse. My grades were borderline, and the teacher was toying with the idea of keeping me back a year. I knew I wasn't failing, but why fight? When Mom made an appointment with my school counselor, I figured I'd really bought it this time.

I waited for her in the hallway. She came out of the meeting looking grim. "We're going to see the vice principal, right now," she said.

Mom didn't kid around. She marched into his office and started in. "You will not keep my son back. I know he can't be failing English. I've seen his work."

Mom was *defending* me!

The vice principal made it clear he thought Mom was making a fuss because she was a famous author and was embarrassed that her son might fail English. But Mom told him she'd kept all my test papers, knew the grade was wrong, and she wasn't leaving his office until it was all sorted out. In the end it turned out that my mom was right. Somehow, my teacher had gotten my grades mixed up and had wrongly averaged them into an F.

Mom and I didn't talk on the way home. I knew she was upset, but all I could think was how she'd fought for me, and believed in me. Mom didn't think I was bad.

"We won," she said as we trailed into the kitchen. It was quiet, so quiet. There was only me and Mom in the house. I couldn't even hear the birds. Her face was soft and smiley as she looked at me. No anger, no skepticism, no mistrust. My mom loved me. She was there for me. She hadn't left me.

"Mom, what did I do that made Dad go away? And I know it was my fault that Grandpa and Grandma left us."

My words surprised me. They had tumbled out unbidden, from someplace inside, someplace I'd denied and ignored. I hadn't been able to face that Dad had left because of me. And I didn't know what I'd done wrong to drive Grandpa and Grandma and my cousin away.

Mom's face registered total surprise. Then she hugged me like when I was little and she could still pick me up. "Your fault? Where did you ever get that? First of all, your father divorced me. Do you hear? *Me.* Not you. He loves you. It's just that he and I didn't get along after a while, and we thought it best for all of us if we parted. As for Grandpa and Grandma, you know the house here was too big for them, and they couldn't take the winters anymore. They didn't leave because of you. Wherever did you get that from?"

That's when I cried. I didn't care if I was too old for that stuff. It felt good to release all the pain I'd been carrying around for the past few months. And I knew it was all right with Mom. She just kept her arms around me while I let it all out.

Then Mom told me it was okay to hurt, but that I must remember to find the joy in each day. She told me it was no good to dwell on the past. I had to learn to let go. Most of all, she told me that she and Dad and my grandparents loved me and nothing I had ever done or might do could take that away.

It took a while, but with Mom's help I was able to stop feeling angry and abandoned by everyone, stop feeling that my parents' divorce was my fault. As I gradually let go of the hidden guilt, my destructive behavior slid away.

Those moments in the kitchen that afternoon have never left me. They never will

To others, my Mom is the glamorous author with her picture on the back cover and her name on the *New York Times* bestseller lists. But to me, she's Mom—my best friend in the world.

Dan's mother is Nora Roberts, bestselling author of such acclaimed novels as Montana Sky. *Dan is a student, living independently (but not too far from) his beloved mountain home and his mom.*

Faith

Faith is the bird that feels the light when the dawn is still dark.

—Rabindranath Tagore

The Search

By D. J. Higo, *48, writer*

~~~~~~

$\mathcal{M}$Y FOSTER MOTHER TOSSED MY BROTHER TOMMY'S diaper toward the pail. It fell short, landing on her new beige carpet. She turned on me, fuming. "You stupid little brat. Look what you made me do."

What had I done? I hadn't touched it or her. I ducked away from the open hand aimed at my face, but too late. My ear stung and my cheek burned.

I was four years old, and Tommy was two something. My brother and I had been in foster care for more than a year. We'd lived with Grandma and Grandpa once, but were taken away because of a custody battle. I didn't know what that meant. All I knew was that Tommy was the only person left who loved me.

That afternoon, the doorbell rang. I flung it wide, and the lady said, "Hi, Donna Jean. Do you remember me? I'm your caseworker."

She had come to take me away. My essence drained like a vial being emptied, and I did the only thing I could—I hid under my bed. I waited, but she didn't come. Finally, I stuck my head out.

Nothing. I tiptoed toward the front door. The caseworker was standing by her car, with Tommy in her arms.

"Wait. Wait!" I screamed, as I ran out the door. "Where are you taking my brother?"

The caseworker pulled out of the driveway, and the last thing I saw was Tommy's face and hands pressed against the glass. His lips formed my name. *Donna Jean. Donna Jean.* And he was crying.

For days after, I sat in the dirty crawl space under the front porch, wondering why I was so horrible that no one wanted me. I rocked and cooed to the bundled-up skirt of my dress, holding it to my chest—my hollow Tommy.

I vowed to remember his name, harboring it in a secret place deep inside of me. There was something else I harbored, a small, stuffed, black dog he left behind. The toy had twinkling, hazel-green eyes, just like my brother's.

Then one day my foster mother packed my suitcase again. Sure enough, there was a knock on the door, and my caseworker was standing on the step. As she took my hand to leave, my foster mother tried to snatch Tommy's toy out of my arms.

Like a wild animal protecting its cub, I held onto the front legs while she jerked and pulled on the hindquarters. "No, no. It's mine," I screamed. There was a loud *pop.* Then a *rrrip.* White stuffing emerged from the dog's underbelly.

The caseworker broke up the tug-of-war. "Let the child have the dog. Today of all days I don't want her upset."

I sniffled all the way to the car. Then it hit me. I wouldn't have to come back to this house again. I brightened with another thought. "Am I going to see Tommy?"

"No, honey. You're going to your new home."

"But . . . but . . . won't Tommy be there?"

"No."

"Then I won't go!"

"You have to, you're being adopted by those nice people we visited several weeks ago. Remember? The ones with the older sister? You said it would be nice to have an older sister."

"Where's Tommy? I want to go with Tommy. Please, please."

"He went back to his father."

"But isn't he my daddy, too? Why can't I go?"

"Because you've been adopted. You're very lucky."

Lucky. That was a funny word to describe my fate. The streets slid by, blurred by my tears. Clutching Tommy's wounded dog, I followed the caseworker up the steps to an open door and waiting arms. This lady had rosy cheeks and wire-rimmed glasses, just like Mrs. Santa Claus. Her hand reached toward my head, and I cringed, waiting for the pain. Instead, gentle fingers stroked my hair. "What have you got there?" she asked.

I tentatively held out the dog. "Aw, its okay, honey. We can fix your puppy." Immediately, she pulled out a sewing basket. I tightened my grip on my precious toy. "It's all right, I won't take it from you. Why don't you hold it while I mend it?"

This was my introduction to the Boltens: Mom, Dad, and my new sister, Sarah. I wanted to be as open and loving toward them as they were toward me. But I couldn't conquer rejection and abuse overnight.

So I clung to Tommy's memory. My brother's golden hair became the stuff of my dreams, the gilded child who was endlessly at my side. We were like Peter Pan and Wendy, the forever little boy and his protective, older sister. He became my invisible companion. We climbed trees, rode my tricycle together, and I taught him how to swim in the blue plastic pool. I even wrote him a note, then buried it under a lilac tree in the backyard. "Dear Tommy, I love you, and will find you when I get big. Love, your sister."

But as I neared my teenage years, I found myself happy with my new family—a mom and dad who smiled when they saw me, and a sister who shared secrets and friends—and Tommy's presence dimmed. At thirteen I was wrapped up in being pretty and accepted by my peers. But I was still saddled with a self-image that languished at the bottom of a barrel.

Perhaps, I thought, *if I knew where I came from, who my family was, and why they didn't keep me, I'd feel better.* I hemmed and hawed, trying to figure out a tactful way to approach the subject without upsetting the only real mother I had ever known.

"Please, Mom, tell me why my other family let me go?"

Her eyes widened, and she hesitated, as if grappling for time. "Other family? Why are you so concerned about this now?"

"I don't know."

"I really don't know much either." She bowed her head for a moment, then stared at me over her glasses. "I do know that some of your ancestors came from England. Let's see, I think there was a great aunt who was a lady-in-waiting to Queen Victoria. I can't remember much more than that."

"What's a lady-in-waiting?"

"To wait on the Queen you must have royal blood, or be married to a duke, or something like that. I'm not too sure."

"Wow!" This was great news. Lady-in-waiting for Queen Victoria? Could it be my royal family didn't know where I was? That must be it. A part of me was relieved. It wasn't that I was unloved, or had been a bad little girl. I had been kidnapped! I was the modern-day version of *The Prince and the Pauper.* Or, I should say, *The Princess and the Pauper.*

And Princess with a capital P is what I became. I put my hair in a French twist like Grace Kelly, dressed in my best clothes, and paraded around with my nose in the air. My mother, father, and Sarah suffered the regal attitude throughout my teenage years. Mom let it go, knowing it was only a Band-Aid. But when I was nineteen, she realized that I was old enough for the truth.

She contacted the attorney who handled my adoption. According to his report, my birth mother, Dorothy, was a waitress. She was sixteen when I was born, but had disappeared and couldn't be found. Her parents were dead. She did come from Anglo-Saxon stock, but five generations ago and with not a drop of royal blood. So I wasn't the queen's daughter. Well, that's okay, sort of. There was still the king, wasn't there?

My father of record, Victor, and his sister, Natally, were still alive. They were of Russian descent. Victor was a window washer, and Natally a housewife. The letter explained that I really wasn't Victor's child. He and Dorothy were married when she was six months pregnant, and she never revealed my real father's name. A year and a half after my birth, a son was born to them—Thomas, my Tommy.

Later, Victor sued for divorce and custody of both of us, citing Dorothy's frequent absences, which made her an unfit mother. Tommy and I were placed in foster care during the lengthy court hearings. In the end, he was returned to his father. I was not.

So much for royalty, important persons, and being the lost princess. I was a nobody. The daughter of a waitress who couldn't be found, and a man who couldn't be named.

On that day I entombed my past and its accompanying desolation under plate armor. I ran from my memories for the next twenty years. More than anything, I ran from the warring parts of my personality—the outward submissiveness, the inward aggression and rebellion, the desire to trust but fear of being hurt. Who was the real me?

Then I met and married a man who reveled in my paradoxical nature. Under Norman's gentle tutelage, my self-esteem flourished. But there was one problem with that kind of love. My plate armor developed cracks. Memories of Tommy seeped through. When the protective shell fell away, in yesterday's mirror I saw my brother's youthful face.

One evening I said to Norman, "You know, I think I would like to search for Tommy. Find out where he is."

"Honey, you do whatever you need for your own happiness."

With a champion like my husband, I had nothing to lose. I contacted Illinois Children's Services, the agency that had handled my adoption, and set up an appointment. I had no idea how I was going to drag out the cloistered information as to my brother's whereabouts, but cough it up they would if I had anything to say about it. After all, Wendy would never let her Peter languish without his older sister.

The post-adoption supervisor and I closeted ourselves in her tiny office. She picked up a folder two inches thick. "This tome is your file. Everything we know about you and Tommy is in here."

"Can I see it?"

"No. We're not allowed to give out any specific information."

"Then how am I supposed to learn anything?"

"Well, you can ask me questions, and if you're right I can't lie to you."

"Good! Then we'll sit here and play twenty, forty, or a hundred questions until I get my answers. Let's start with my mother's birth date. Was she born between January and June?"

"No."

"Between July and December?"

"Yes"

We played the silly game for hours, until I had the dates and addresses I needed. She wished me luck and gave me the name of a locator agency that had been successful for other adoptees. I didn't need an agency, I was going to find Neverland on my own.

It made sense to start with my grandparents, since the agency didn't have a clue as to the whereabouts of my brother or step-father. Grandpa and Grandma had died several years earlier, so my first call was to the funeral home. "Hi, my name is Donna Higo. You don't know me, but you buried my biological grand-parents." He didn't have to know the truth. "I'm searching for my brother, Tommy Mironovka, and I'm hoping your records might give an address for a next of kin."

"Give me the name again, and I'll look it up." I mentally crossed all my fingers and toes until he came back, "I show the next of kin as a Natally."

"That's my aunt. Can you give me her last name and phone number? She has to know where Tommy is."

"I'm sorry, dear, but I can't give out private information."

"You don't know what this means to me. Please."

"Well, I shouldn't do this, but I'll try the number I have, and if I reach your aunt, I'll give her your message."

"Thank you."

The rest of the afternoon and evening dragged by with no phone call. The following afternoon I called him back. "This is Donna Higo. Were you able to find my aunt?"

"Yes, but I'm not sure you want to hear what I have to say."

"What do you mean?"

"I left your number on your aunt's answering machine and she called me this morning. She asked what you wanted. I said to get in touch with your brother. She asked if you sounded normal, like you were drunk or on drugs, or something."

I felt outraged. This woman didn't even know me. "What did you say?"

"Normal."

"So what happened?"

"She said she'd thrown your number away. And I didn't keep it either."

"That's no problem, I'll give it to you again. It's—"

"Hold on a minute, I'm not finished. Before she hung up, she told me not to bother her again. Then your brother called. He sounded frantic when I told him we didn't have your number. 'This is my sister, my real sister,' he said, and he begged me to search the garbage cans, but the trash had gone out already."

"But you got Tommy's number?"

"No. I didn't think of it. But don't hang up yet, I still had the message pad where I'd written your number, so I lightly penciled over the indentation. The last two digits were faint, and I'm not sure I gave him it to him right."

Faint. Tommy and I were reaching out for each other, only to shake hands through a man with a shroud. I racked my brain, then said, "Couldn't you put my telephone number in my grandparents' file? That way, if he calls back you can give it to him properly."

"I'm sorry, Mrs. Higo, but I'm beginning to feel like I'm in the center of some family problem."

"Please. You know Tommy and I are trying to find each other."

"Sorry."

Why did I think this was going to be so easy? I was so close to that needle in the haystack, so close it had pricked me. I had a few more days left before I had to return home, so I plunked myself down next to the phone, just in case.

I was staying with my sister, Sarah. That night she'd arranged to have dinner with friends. "Come with us," she said.

"I'm not in the mood."

"Are you going to sit by the phone the rest of your life?"

"Maybe."

"Oh, for God's sake, Donna, you have to face reality. You've done the best you could, but Tommy isn't going to call, honey. He's never going to call. If you stay here, all you'll do is cry."

So I went with Sarah and her friends and sat dull-eyed and miserable. We returned home sometime after midnight, and I went to my room, although I was far from sleep.

"Donna, come here."

I hurried to my sister, and she silently pointed to the message button on her answering machine.

I pressed it. A male voice filled the room. "If this is where Donna Jean is, please have her call me. This is Tom."

"Oh, my God!" My brother's voice. It was so deep. My brother's voice! I reached for the phone.

Sarah grabbed it out of my hand. "Honey, I know how excited you are, but it's almost 1 A.M. Wait 'til morning."

"But Tommy . . ."

"He'll still be there in the morning."

I curled up in bed, thinking about the golden-haired little boy and the deep voice I heard on the machine. For the first time, I began to think of Tommy as Tom, a man. My God, would I recognize him? Is his hair still golden? Does he look anything like me? I didn't know anything about him, what kind of man was he? My mind rolled with questions the rest of that sleepless, glorious night.

Shortly after the sun rose, I phoned.

"Donna Jean, Donna Jean, where have you been?"

I closed my eyes, the better to savor Tommy's voice.

"Neverland, Tommy," I said, although I knew he wouldn't understand. "I've been waiting for you in Neverland."

Four years have passed since Donna and Tom were reunited, and Donna's family has grown to include three beautiful nieces and a grand-nephew. But her sister-in-law, Joyce, holds a special place in her heart, because she stuck by Tommy's side while he worked through his own rejection demons. Today Donna and Tommy have a very special bond that the years of separation never diminished.

The Miracle of Prayer

By Liz Kolshak, 11

THE PHEASANTS ARE OUR GOOD FRIENDS, MORE LIKE FAMILY. My dad and Mr. Pheasant were both in the Marines, and my mom and Mrs. Pheasant are both named Ann and very close. My older sisters and I are friends with Katie and Sara, the Pheasants' twin girls. Mom says that when you're in the military, your friends become like your family because you have to support each other.

One Sunday we returned from church and Mr. Pheasant called to tell us that Sara was in the hospital. At first I thought maybe my friend had broken her arm, but when Mom and Dad told my sister and me that they had to go to the hospital, I figured it was bad. My parents didn't say much, except that Sara was unconscious and an ambulance came for her.

"Say a prayer for Sara," Mom said before she left.

"Please, God," I prayed, "let Sara be all right."

My parents were at the hospital all day. Finally, they called and talked to my sister. She got real upset and said Mom and Dad had asked her not to tell me about Sara—except she did. My friend was very sick and was probably going to die. *Die? She was only eleven. How could this be happening?*

I didn't move. I couldn't. "Please God, don't let Sara die."

When Mom and Dad came home that night, they only spoke if we asked them a question, and I could see that their eyes were red.

"Can I help?" I asked.

"Why don't you say a prayer," Mom answered.

I talked to God that night, and asked Him to help my friend. I hoped He had heard me, but how could I know?

My mom's a nurse, and she stayed with Mrs. Pheasant in the hospital almost all the time for the next three weeks. She dropped everything to help, so my sisters and I tried to pitch in around the house.

And every day and every night, I prayed.

Katie came to stay with us and told me what had happened the night her twin became sick. Sara had been baby-sitting for her neighbor. She was fine when she came home and played with Katie and another friend who was sleeping over that night. But about eleven o'clock Sara told her mom that her neck hurt, and Mrs. Pheasant said, "Go to bed, you'll be okay."

An hour later Sara vomited some blood. She usually was the one who got sick, so her mom thought it was just the flu that was going around. Mrs. Pheasant cleaned her up and put her back in bed, and her dad lay down with her in case she felt sick again.

At one o'clock, Mr. Pheasant was awakened by the sound of Sara gurgling. Katie woke up when her mom started screaming and crying. "Gary, is she dead? Is she dead?" Katie heard them call 911 to get Sara to the hospital.

It turned out that Sara had something called AVM, where the arteries and veins in her brain had not properly formed. She'd had this condition since birth, but nobody knew it. Mom explained that sometimes people live their whole lives not knowing anything's wrong, and sometimes the veins and arteries burst. That's what happened to Sara. Now she needed an operation on her brain, but was too weak.

"It's like Sara's sitting on a fence post," Mom said. "If she falls one way, she'll die, but if she falls another, she'll live."

My family and I prayed for Sara all the time. When we said our blessing before our meals, we prayed for her. When Mom and Dad took us to church for a special service, we prayed for her, and people in Sara's parish helped pass out pink bows for people to stick in their car or windows to remind them to pray for Sara, too.

It took one week before she was strong enough for surgery. Katie stayed at our house again, so we were all together during it. When the phone rang with the news that Sara's operation was successful, Katie was happy and so were we.

That night, my prayers changed a little. This time I said thank you.

That was last year, and Sara has had a full recovery. You'd never know she'd had brain surgery if she didn't have short hair.

To this day we thank God for keeping Sara alive. This story proves there is a God, and when you pray to Him, He will answer.

Sara now wears her hair any length she fancies, and enjoys her good health and good fortune. Liz is entering seventh grade, and Sara and she are still close friends.

Mending Hearts

From Claudia Kerr, 42, publisher,
Outlet Shopping Guides for the Midwest and California

THE ONLY SOUND PENETRATING MY AWARENESS WAS THE muted rush of wind as I defied the speed limit to reach a stricken father too many miles across town.

Unhappiness had been my lot these last few years, culminating twelve months before in my divorce from a man I had loved dearly for a decade. Now my seemingly healthy, smiling father—a robust, hardheaded Swede—lay in a hospital bed, felled by a heart attack.

I pulled my attention to the road. Only ten blocks to Mercy Hospital. I pressed harder on the accelerator until the familiar outline of the medical center that served our small town came into sight. Once inside, the elevator took forever to rise to the second-floor Cardiac Intensive Care Unit.

"Calm down, ma'am." The nurse at the central reception area looked as if she were familiar with the wild-eyed, frantic women whose species I had joined today. "You're a member of Mr. Anderson's family? You realize only family members are allowed in ICU, and then only for a few moments."

"I'm his daughter Claudia. Before I go in, can you tell me his condition?"

"He appears to have suffered a heart attack. The doctors are awaiting test results to confirm this. He's resting comfortably." As she spoke she waved me toward a door with one hand and scooped up a chart with another.

One fluid turn, and she glided away—efficiency in motion.

I stared at the glass window and door she had indicated. An eerie green light emanated from within as if the room itself were under water. When I opened the door, the low swish of oxygen and the beeping rhythm of my father's damaged heart stopped me momentarily. I didn't want to be alone when I faced my dad laid low and helpless, attached to every machine the hospital could round up. But my mother and siblings hadn't arrived yet. I was alone. I took a deep breath and stepped into the room.

Dad looked so small, his face tightened under a drug-induced sleep, his poor body covered in tubes and bands. I slipped his hand between my own and studied him. So intent was my focus, it took me a moment to notice the two other men in the room. They had their backs to me, their heads close in consultation, the one listening to the doctor in his white coat.

My God, it's Jeff. It's Jeff! What's he doing here?

The man who had been my husband turned as if he could read my mind. He closed the distance between us in three strides. One arm slipped around my shoulders, another around my waist as I stood stiff with surprise. He hugged me quickly, then led me to the doctor.

"This is the cardiac resident. He's told me your dad's EKG indicates extensive damage."

"What does that mean?" I gasped.

"I'm afraid he's suffered a major heart attack. We were just discussing options."

My worst fears were confirmed. *My poor dad. Please, God. Help my poor dad.* I almost lost my presence of mind until Jeff's sympathetic touch grounded me again with a spark of anger.

"How did you know?" It was an accusation, not a question.

"Somehow they had your old number. Our number, Claud. I gave them the correct one and got over here before anyone else."

In the businesslike manner I remembered so well, Jeff got right back to the doctor. Did he have any idea of the extent of damage? When would an angiogram be performed? Was there a possibility of angioplasty? If surgery were necessary, how long would it take? Two hours? Ten? When would it be performed? Did we have time for a second opinion?

I listened to Jeff's careful questions. I'd always said that our story was like something that always happens to someone else, not me. He'd walked into my office ten years before when I was a single parent selling advertising. And it was love at first sight . . . for both of us.

But it had been a long twelve months since Jeff and I were divorced. Although Jeff explained his reasons, I could never fully understand them. Or accept them. Nevertheless, in the legal system dissolution was final.

I had adjusted quite well to the realities of a situation not of my choosing. Without my family, friends, and God's help, I don't think I could have made it. I thought I'd overcome the bewilderment and hurt of losing my husband. But seeing Jeff again so unexpectedly at so vulnerable an emotional time, I knew I hadn't . . . not really.

A surge of anger tore through the shock. *Jeff shouldn't be here. He's not my family anymore. He gave up that right.*

"I'm calling the university, Claudia," Jeff said as soon as he'd finished his cross-examination. "Your dad's going to have the best cardiac specialist I can find." With that, he strode from the room, leaving me disarmed and speechless.

A moan from my poor father erased away any thoughts of Jeff or myself, and I bent over him, praying as hard as I could. I don't know how long I sat there before the nurse shooed me away. Not long enough.

I lingered outside, watching Dad through the window. The feel of a friendly arm around my waist startled me.

"I've already called in the best for your dad," Jeff murmured. "I'm here for you, Claud. However long it takes."

I'm here for you. However long it takes. I'd heard those words before. The greens and grays of my father's room faded into the antiseptic whites of the maternity ward of years past. And I saw Jeff as he had been then, overwhelmed with a shared grief.

➤➤➤–•–◄◄◄

He'd been waiting for me when I came out of the recovery room after my daughter's stillbirth. I must have slept—I don't remember—because I woke to see my husband cradling a bundle dressed in a pink nightie and hat and wrapped in a pink blanket.

"I don't want to see it," I protested. "We have three healthy children. I don't want to see it."

"We have *four* children, Claudia," Jeff said gently. "She's ours. Dead or alive, she's ours, and we should acknowledge her."

113

I wanted to protest, turn away, but his face was soft and sad and instead I reached out. He placed our daughter in my arms.

"I'm here for you, Claud. We'll stay here until you feel comfortable with saying good-bye. I'm here for you. However long it takes."

And he was.

—→→→ • ←←←—

"You okay?" Jeff's voice brought me back to the present.

I nodded.

"Your mom, sister, and brother are on their way up." He hesitated. "Your dad's going to be fine, you know. He's made of tough stuff."

"Thank you, Jeff," I said. And I meant it.

It was a long, long day. My brother, my sister, my mother, and I kept vigil, gratefully snatching the few moments we were allowed with my father.

And Jeff was there for us. He brought us food when he saw we were hungry. He asked the doctors questions we couldn't think of in our shock. He infused us with hope by his very presence.

When they wheeled Dad into surgery for a quadruple bypass, Jeff brushed his fingers along my father's brawny hand, and Dad smiled.

I had a lot of time to think during those interminable hours of not knowing. Dad's operation was a success, but it took until late the next day before we knew he was out of danger and in recovery. Jeff, my family, and I prayed together when word came.

The quiet words to God soothed me, and suddenly I remembered every happy hour of my childhood. I also remembered the joyous times with the man who held our hands and bowed his head with us in giving thanks.

I was grateful for Jeff's presence, his strength, his support. Barriers I wasn't aware I'd built were breached, and for the first time in over a year I found I could see this man again as the good person, father, and friend he'd always been.

It struck me in the quiet of Mercy Hospital that love has many faces. In this turbulent world of ours, it should be embraced and cherished wherever we can find it. Jeff was no longer my husband. Nor did I want that. I had no desire to go back to the past when the future looked so bright again. He was still my friend and I could cherish that.

"God makes you better, not bitter," I whispered at the end of our prayer.

"What did you say, Claud?" Jeff asked.

"You remember. God makes you better, not bitter."

He smiled. "How could I forget? Don't let go of that."

I smiled back. God, in His infinite wisdom, had shown me how to be stronger, how to recognize His gifts even in guises we might not want to accept. Love doesn't have to die in bitterness. It doesn't have to languish in regret. Those stunt the soul. Love opens the door to other love.

My healing, along with my father's, had begun.

→→→ • ←←←

Four years later, Claudia's father enjoys life as a healthy, robust man. Claudia and Jeff are still special friends. They always will be.

Sixty-Two Years

Overheard at the Ana Hotel Health Club, Washington, D.C.
Name withheld by request

᚜᚜᚜᚜᚜

HIS DENSE, SILVER-WHITE HAIR WAS CUT CLOSE TO THE scalp in the European way. His Italian suit was impeccably cut to subtly disguise a slight bulge at the tummy, common to men accustomed to a certain fine lifestyle. He wasn't wearing a wedding ring.

He sat quietly, reading the *Wall Street Journal,* and there was something more than his easy aura of power that made me think I recognized him. But the name wouldn't come.

The door to the women's locker room opened and a slender redhead bounced out, still clad in the leotards that showed her dedication to the American dream body. Her eyes passed over me unseeing as she scanned the small foyer. Without hesitation, she strode to the distinguished gentleman.

"Paul? Paul . . . ?"

I didn't catch the last name.

"Yes?" He closed his paper, and rested it on his knee.

"You don't know me. I'm Melissa. I'm afraid I kept Maggie talking while we were getting changed—I needed some advice."

She spread out pale, freckled hands in apology. "She'll be about ten minutes. She just wanted me to tell you."

The man nodded, and the smile that softened a face that acknowledged its tenure in the world of business made me wish I was Maggie.

"I've been waiting for that lady for sixty-two years," he said. "Ten minutes more is nothing."

A soft sigh whispered past Melissa's lips. "Oh," she said. "Oh, how lovely."

As I watched her walk away, a slightly disheveled, not unattractive brown-haired woman in her late forties rushed out of the locker room and straight to the man two chairs away from me.

He stood immediately and she leaned into his arms, oblivious to who might be watching. "I'm sorry, love, I met this girl, Melissa, did she tell you . . . ?"

"Yes," he said, and I was almost embarrassed by the look that passed between them. It was more than love. It encompassed understanding, trust, the contentment of two people who had found each other at last.

>>>-•-<<<

Washington is a small town, and I see Maggie and Paul about now and then. I watch them hold hands as they walk into a restaurant, see them touch, and smile at each other across a table. I strain to hear the low murmur of two people in soft conversation. Lately, I noticed they are both wearing wedding rings. Nothing ostentatious. Just two plain hands that declare their commitment.

I am in my forties, unattached. There have been times I dated men I shouldn't have, sometimes, I admit, out of loneliness. But I don't do that anymore. It seems that every time I am about to make that mistake, I see Maggie and Paul together somewhere. And I look at them and take hope.

I am willing to wait for it to be for me as it is for this couple, who serve as my talismans. But if my true companion and I never find each other, I'm not willing to compromise anymore. I have too much self-respect to accept less.

→→→• ←←←

The storyteller says that it's been seven years since she first saw Maggie and Paul. She reports they are still glowing, and she is now dating a man she trusts, loves, and admires. She blesses the special afternoon she was sitting in the foyer of the Ana Hotel Health Club waiting for a friend—who was also late.

Quiet
Miracles

*The single word,
the lightest touch, the
simplest truth . . . all can
produce miracles.*

—Anonymous

I Love You

From Sandra Israel, 54, Aspen Chapter emeritus, Komen Foundation

LIKED TO THINK I WAS DIFFERENT FROM MOST OF MY colleagues who came of age in the early 1960s. Our generation was still imbued with the values and ideals of an earlier decade that worshiped the traditional marriage and promised happily-ever-after would follow. While the women's liberation movement was burning bras and struggling for recognition, I had attained the new dream of every radical young woman of my era: a job and independence.

Did I say a job, as if it were merely a nine-to-five routine office position? Far from it. I had been recruited by Vice President Hubert Humphrey to be one of his personal assistants. My days were crammed with the excitement of the White House and political Washington, D.C., trips to Africa and Israel and every major city in the nation. In '66 I was twenty-six, a hick from Missouri who'd made good. Marriage was not going to spoil my life.

But he was a handsome, blue-eyed charmer, and I was too young to differentiate between truth and passion. We married. Then I made the classic mistake: I traded in the job I loved for the ephemeral promises of security and love everlasting.

My divorce was bred out of disappointments and dismay at the realities of life with the man I'd promised forever. Like so many women back then, I probably would have stuck with a relationship we might now define as abusive, if only for the children's sake—Rachel, born in 1969, and Josh, born in 1971. But my husband did me a favor. When Josh was six months old, he cleared out the bank account and disappeared.

Nixon reigned in the White House now. My mentor had long gone, and so had my erstwhile friends and connections. I had burned my bridges too well. But if I was bitter about giving up a dream career, I never, ever regretted the one gift from my brief three-and-a-half-year marriage—my children.

How I loved them and how they loved me. Rachel and Josh didn't seem to mind when the three of us jammed ourselves into a one-bedroom apartment, or that I rotated through a procession of dismally paying jobs that left me tired and irritable. My son would crawl into my lap the minute I'd come home, wrap his arms around my neck, and stay there all night if I'd let him.

And Rachel would watch with knowing eyes beyond her years and take Josh from my arms so I could get dinner—macaroni and cheese with applesauce again. "It's okay, Ma," she'd say, already understanding the guilt of all single mothers.

My daughter was as close as a joined twin to her brother. I couldn't decipher Josh's early mumbles but Rachel could. "He wants a cookie, Mom," she'd say with authority. It was my five-year-old daughter who brought to my attention that her brother had hearing problems. No wonder at two he still wasn't forming clear words.

Pride had kept me in Washington. I didn't want to go home to "I told you so." But Josh needed help. My father argued that I could live on less in Kansas City, and he would co-sign on the lease of a livable apartment for us. "But that's all we can do, Sandy. We're just common folk, not like those glamorous friends of yours back East."

Stock market blues, inflation, no good times anywhere, including the Midwest. I was lonely. It seemed a week couldn't go by without Josh having a cold, and Rachel looked more wan than robust. Maybe my mother was right about my children, they should live with her. At least she was home all day and could be a proper mother, whatever that was supposed to mean.

I'd resisted because I felt my parents were too old for youngsters, especially a son with the extra attention and care Josh needed. But mostly, it was because my memory of my mother was of a woman I could never please.

Maybe it was the accumulation of months, going into years, of disappointments. It didn't seem to matter what I did, it never worked. I'd thought things were looking up when I got a sales job at a local television station. After all, I was the first woman they'd ever hired.

I didn't care that I was given all the accounts the guys couldn't squeeze any business from. What hurt more were the snide remarks—"we know how you got *that* account." Always there were the few loud voices at the coffee machine discussing the woman who wore a suit because it might make her more like a man. Then there was the sabotage—my presentation for a new client unaccountably missing just before a meeting. This and my worries about Rachel and Josh were what ground me down every day.

This particular wintry afternoon was gray and bleak, matching my spiralling mood. I'd spent months building up my account list and finally, today, I was to land my first big account—or so I thought.

As I picked up my portfolio and prepared to leave for the closing, my superior beckoned me into his office. My colleague was sitting next to his desk.

"Sandra, your client called this morning and said he wants to go with your ideas, but he'd rather work with Peters."

I looked at Peters' smug, jowly face across the room. For some silly reason, all I could see was the obscene white pimple protruding through the thinning hair on his forehead. I clutched my presentation like a shield.

"He's never talked with the man. He has no notion of the campaign we've put together."

My boss shrugged and turned away in dismissal, without even the courtesy of an explanation. Peters laced and unlaced thick fingers on his lap. I suddenly realized what was going on. If I snagged this account, I'd be making as much money as this guy who'd been at the station for five years.

My boss swung around when I opened the door to leave. He had his hand out. "The paperwork?"

"What paperwork?" I walked out of the room.

I drove more slowly than usual to pick up Rachel and Josh from preschool. My jaw was hurting again. "Stress," the dentist had told me when I couldn't open my mouth wide enough for a sandwich. "You've got to change your lifestyle." *Sure doc, could you tell me how?*

The kids and I let ourselves into the empty apartment that seemed to get colder by the day. Rachel took my hand when I'd hung up our coats. "Josh has something he wants to say to you, Ma."

"But I can't understand him, honey."

She didn't answer, just led us both into the living room, where my son had sat himself in the middle of the floor, clutching his teddy bear. His nose was running again. I knelt beside him, Kleenex in hand, and wiped it clean. He smiled up at me with bright, expectant eyes. "I lul lu, Mama," he said.

I love you. My boy was telling me he loved me. My serious Rachel gave her brother a little prod in the back. Josh's baby-smooth forehead puckered with concentration. "You—you are pwetty."

The three of us clung together like we were in a lifeboat on some empty ocean. "I lul lu, Mama," Josh repeated until he couldn't keep his blue eyes open any more, and fell asleep with his head in my lap.

I took him to work with me the next day because he was too sick for daycare and there was no one to watch him. I got fired on the spot. That was all right, I needed to stay home with my son for a few days.

Things got better from then on. I got a job in sales at WDAS, the top-rated radio station in town. Again I got the client list nobody wanted, but I went to work and came home every day to Josh's now-perfect "I love you, Mama. You are so beautiful."

Such simple words, but they got me through the next few years. They gave me the courage to pull out of Kansas City and move us all to a small town in Colorado where the air was cleaner, the schools better, the streets safer, and I was offered a job as sales manager at the local radio station.

Josh and Rachel were babies when they helped me so long ago. I think my son knew on some instinctive level what his words meant. For years he never let a day go by without telling me he loved me.

He still calls every week, no matter where he may be. "I love you, Mama. You are so beautiful," are the last words I hear before he hangs up the phone. And I still smile.

→→→ • ←←←

Josh is twenty-five and making a way for himself in California. Rachel majored in international affairs and Japanese in college. Her goal is to work for a multinational company with offices in Tokyo. Sandra recently got married to her soulmate. In 1990, she was the prime mover in starting the Aspen chapter of the Komen Foundation, a leader in the fight against breast cancer.

Is There a Doctor on the Plane?

From Marcelline Vozzella, 10

※※※※

$\mathcal{I}$ LIKE TO TELL THIS STORY BECAUSE IT ALWAYS MAKES ME FEEL proud. Dad saved a man from dying on a plane, and I saw it.

My father is a doctor, and I know he has helped many people sick with cancer. He works real hard, so it's a treat for the whole family when he can take a vacation.

One night, we were in a plane coming home from a trip. Halfway home, we heard an announcement from the captain: "Is there a doctor on board?"

My mom and dad were asleep, and I didn't want to wake them up, but I couldn't see anyone else moving to answer the call.

"Please, are there any doctors on board?"

Daddy was snoring, so I tugged on his sleeve. He snorted, and turned his head on the pillow. I tugged on him again. His teeth ground, but he didn't wake up. "Dad! Dad!" I nagged. Finally, he opened one eye and looked at me, just in time to hear the captain's third rerun of his request. Dad groaned.

By this time Mom was awake, too. Dad turned and caught her eye, and his eyebrows raised as if asking a question.

"If you go," Mom said, "remember you can't make any mistakes. People can be nasty when you try to help and make a mistake."

"I know," Dad answered.

They didn't say another word for a few seconds, then Mom smiled. "You'd better go and see if you can help."

"You know I have to, honey."

I saw him approach the stewardess and talk a few minutes, then he followed her.

"Mom," I said, "Can I go to the bathroom?"

I wanted to go for two reasons. One because I had to go, and two because I wanted to find out more of what was going on. I tiptoed until I could see Dad. He was talking to a man who looked real sick and he was alone with him, so I guess he was the only doctor on the plane . . . or at least the only one with a daughter to wake him up.

Daddy reached down to grasp the man's hand to take his pulse. I moved closer to see better, but Daddy looked up just then, and he was frowning.

I ducked into the bathroom real fast, then turned on the light and everybody can guess what I did next. When I came out, the stewardess had brought oxygen, and Dad had placed a mask over the man's nose and mouth. I knew from the look on Daddy's face that this was serious. I got scared and went back to my seat.

A little later, Dad walked by us and disappeared through the curtain that separated us from first class.

"He's going to talk to the captain," Mom told me.

I don't know what he said, but the captain announced we had an emergency, and he must land the plane. When we got to the ground, they put the man on a stretcher and my dad stayed with him until he was safe in the ambulance waiting outside.

Finally, Daddy came back. He closed his eyes, and I knew he was tired, but I wanted to know so bad what had happened.

"It was a myocardial infarction," he said. "A bad one."

"A heart attack," Mom whispered to me.

"Poor guy would have been better off with a paramedic who deals with this kind of thing every day. The last time I treated an MI was during my internship." He sighed and shook his head. "At least the ambulance was equipped with the right stuff."

I remembered Mom and Dad's conversation before Daddy left to answer the captain's call. If something happened to that man, would my father be in trouble? I shouldn't have made him wake up.

Dad put his arm around my shoulder. "You look worried, Princess," he said

"I don't want you to get in trouble," I blurted out.

"Why would I?"

"What if that man dies?"

"He might, but does that mean I shouldn't have tried to help him? No, Princess. Remember the hymn you sing in church on Sunday? 'Whatsoever you do to the least of my brothers, that you do unto Me.' I believe it with all my heart."

"So do I," Mom said. "I'm sorry if our silly conversation made you upset. Your dad didn't have a choice. Neither do any of us when it comes to doing what's right."

Dad went to sleep again, and I rubbed his head because he had a headache . . . he loved that.

After we got home that night, my dad called the hospital and found out that the man with the heart attack had survived. Dad had saved him, and given him an extra chance at life.

I think about what Mom and Dad said and did on that plane. I think about it a lot. Sometimes kids will try to make me do stupid things, like smoke a cigarette or make silly phone calls, and they make fun of me if I don't. Whenever I'm caught in a situation like that, I think of Mom and Dad.

I hope I have the courage to do what's right, no matter what might happen to me because of it.

→→→• ←←←

Marcelline is an outgoing fifth-grader with a passel of friends. She loves basketball and softball and has a gift for mathematics that leaves her family in awe.

Her Only Coat

From Dorothy Vance, 70s, homemaker, as told to
and written by Dawn Miller, 30, author, The Journal of Callie Wade

꧁꧂

THERE'S AN OLD SAYING THAT GOES, "DON'T PRAY FOR AN easier life, pray to be a stronger person." My mama never did have an easy life, bringing seven of us into the world whole and strong, in spite of no doctor to be had for miles. She raised us alone as well— what with my pa gone most of the time, showing up just long enough to gamble away any extra Mama could get picking berries.

But Mama never complained. Even when the Depression hit Missouri, she made sure we never did without. She was so solid. I can still see her plain, gathering wild plums and mushrooms, her auburn hair bleached by endless hours in the sun, laughing and telling us stories as she dyed feed sacks and stitched them into clothes.

Her hands were callused and stiff by years of work. I remember finding a picture later in life of her as a young woman, before she'd married Pa, dressed in fine clothes and lace, her soft white hands resting on her own pa's shoulder, and I couldn't help wondering if she'd ever wished things had been different.

I never voiced it, though. Mama would have laughed it away as foolishness. Sturdy Irish stock is how my brother Woodrow described her. "Proud" was how I saw her. Not the foolish kind of pridefulness. More the satisfying kind that comes from loving well and seeing the labors of that love come back.

It was during the hardest time Mama seemed to shine the most. The winter of '33 was one of those times. The summer floods that year had drowned out what little she had tried to coax from our garden. By December we were running out of food.

That morning I saw something akin to fear in Mama's faded green eyes. It was a look foreign to me, so I watched her close as she stood alone next to the window, staring hard into the distance as if the effort might bring Pa home . . . and with him, some food.

Mama turned away after a while and looked around the room like she was just realizing where she was. "Best get your coats on," she told us quietly, then went to her room and fetched her own.

Some people might have laughed at that coat of Mama's—the brown and black tweed threadbare as it was, with just a little bit of fluff at the collar that once had been some kind of fur—but us girls thought it was a fine coat.

Tall and willowy as Mama was, she turned it into something almost regal-looking. I recall thinking that as I walked alongside of her down the icy road that led away from our house.

None of us said much, though, for we knew where we were headed, and in spite of Mama's forced cheerfulness, I knew she dreaded it as much as us.

Aunt Anne was Pa's oldest sister, and wore that title as if it gave her free reign on Mama. All of Pa's wrongdoings were Mama's fault, and anything she gave to us always came with a price. She was what people called "well-to-do." I guess Mama figured she was our last hope, for I know she wouldn't have endured what she did otherwise.

I'll never forget us standing on that wide front porch, Mama holding the baby on her hip as she tried to shield him from an icy blast of wind. Aunt Anne stood just inside her door, her lips pursed as she gazed at us kids from the warmth of her house.

"My children are hungry. Can you spare some meat?"

"I might have some food. What you got to offer me?"

"I'll clean your house. I'll cook."

"Do that myself. But your coat don't look half bad."

I saw Mama's back go straight. "No, Anne, I guess it don't," she said, and put Leonard down, her eyes soft on the rest of us. She hesitated an instant and her fingers stroked the remains of the poor fur of her collar. "It's all I have." Then she took off her coat and folded it neat before she offered it to Aunt Anne.

I'm not sure what hurt me more—seeing Mama giving up her only coat or knowing my aunt, my own blood, would take it so easily. But those feelings were soon put aside as we labored along side of Mama the ten miles back to our own home.

Horrible cold as it was, there was Mama, walking tall and proud in spite it, Leonard tucked up on one hip while she carried her precious little cut of scrap meat under her other arm.

It wasn't until I was in the warmth of our home that I got to thinking hard about Aunt Anne again, and the coat she took. The more I thought about it, the madder I got. I barely touched my dinner and Mama, never one to miss a thing, came right out and asked why I was so mad.

"Aunt Anne shamed us," I said hotly. "She treated us like beggars, and then took your pride and joy away."

Mama's laugh surprised me. "If anything, she gave it back," she said. "That coat wasn't my pride, Dorothy. You kids are."

Her words have remained with me to this day. In that kitchen of my childhood, with the smells of dinner and firewood filling the room, and the look of content in my mother's eyes, I learned how little the material things really mattered in this life.

———•———

Dorothy, Dawn's grandmother, epitomizes the ancient tradition of oral storytelling. Dawn has found her an inspiration as she attempts in her writing to capture both the cadence of the Midwestern speech and the nuggets of beauty to be found in the harshest of tales.

Aunt Leila

From Simona Chivian, 65, therapist

AUNT LEILA WAS AN OPERA SINGER, A MEZZO-SOPRANO who'd made her operatic debut at the Manhattan Opera House playing Santuzza in *Cavalleria Rusticana* when she was only twenty-three. She was my mother's sister—the glamorous, bohemian member of our family—slightly, just slightly, scandalous.

She wore her hair, which was very black, swept back from her face and gathered into a beautiful chignon at the nape of her neck. She walked like a queen, and wore long flowing capes, while the rest of us were swathed in winter coats. Artists populated her universe, in love with her green eyes and alabaster skin. Their paintings were filled with images of Leila.

My aunt had no children of her own, and it was a very special treat for my sister, my brother, and me to stay with Leila. Her idea of entertaining children would be to sweep us off to parties, plays, and operas, with no thought for a child's proper bedtime, and somehow we always ended the night on Broadway.

This was the 1940s. Upper Broadway was a dynamic, vibrant boulevard, alive with cafes where people would gather to discuss the affairs of the hour, sip Manhattans and strong coffee, and smoke exotic-smelling cigarettes, often cupping them inside the palm in the European way. It was a strange and wondrous land for a little girl, so foreign to my own New Jersey streets.

Leila's apartment was at 79th and Riverside Drive overlooking the Hudson River, a neighborhood where musicians lived and worked. I used to love to walk her small black Scottie dog, because in the spring and summer the windows were always open. As I'd wander the streets, I could hear people vocalizing, their voices climbing and descending scales and octaves. The sound of pianos and violins spilled into the afternoon. Sometimes I felt like I was privy to all the music of the universe.

This was the night-and-day world of my Aunt Leila, the woman who exposed me to music and art, to fashion dictated only by one's own personality, and to free thinking. This was also the woman who, as I was about to enter my teenage years, gave me a very precious gift.

I was eleven and awkward, slouching around with my shoulders hunched as if that could make me disappear. I would examine each and every pore in my face and find it faulty. The mirror was my enemy. I despaired of ever being anything but an ugly duckling.

One afternoon, as I was sitting cross-legged on my bed feeling sorry for myself, Aunt Leila came to call. She and my mother went to the upstairs parlor to visit. It was the room next to mine and I could hear the hum of conversation drifting through the partially open door.

Then I heard my Aunt Leila's voice, trumpet clear. "Anna," she said to my mother, "your daughter, Simona, has the most *beautiful* eyes."

Beautiful? Something about me was beautiful? Did she mean that? I rushed to the mirror. The same deep, brown eyes that I looked at every morning gazed back at me. But wait, didn't they have a slight curve upward, an almost almond shape with perhaps a fleck of gold? I tilted my head to see my suddenly beautiful eyes from a different angle. I hadn't really noticed before, but they *were* sort of . . . lovely.

Aunt Leila's few inspired words were enough for me to live on until I grew into my body, and the ugly duckling started to become a swan.

As I look back now, I understand that Aunt Leila knew how intensely self-conscious I was feeling. She knew I didn't see myself as very pretty at this in-between age. She said something that made me feel, if not gorgeous, at least attractive enough to get through the next couple of years.

I think one of the aspects of caring is the ability to empower others. My aunt gave me a priceless gift. She saw me through the eyes of love.

—————•—————

Leila's legacy lives on. Simona has never lost her love of New York or of music. There's nothing she enjoys more than to listen to cool jazz in a hot club past the midnight hour.

Revelation

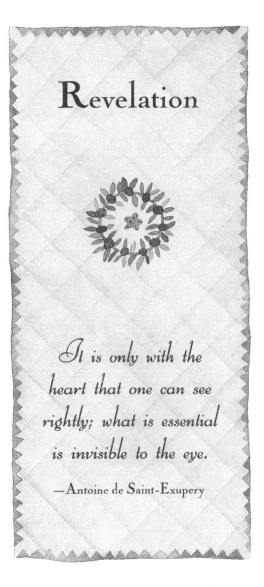

It is only with the heart that one can see rightly; what is essential is invisible to the eye.

—Antoine de Saint-Exupery

Caught in the Crossfire

From Mary Cecilia Waugh, 80s, registered dietitian

W HEN THE TWENTIETH CENTURY WAS YOUNG, AND WORLD War I had just ended, Mom took my brother, sister, and me to Ireland. I was six years old, and we stayed for three years.

It was a time of revolution against England. The Black and Tans, as the English soldiers were called, were a familiar sight in the streets and lanes of Ireland, but I registered little of that. As with all children, I cared for only what touched me, and war did not.

I loved Ireland, with its meadows of shadow green, dotted with clover and yellow buttercups in the spring. Misty gray days would suddenly burst into gold with the rare appearance of the sun. I remember the convent school in which my mother enrolled me, and the caress of sweet air on my face as the nuns passed quietly by in the gloom of the brown stone building.

Closer to my heart were the stories told around Gran's kitchen table, near the peat fire burning on the hearth. Ireland is full of the faery, a fey country of ruins and mists and uncanny places where magic lingers, and the Christian soul flees before ancient pagan spirits.

Many an evening I was regaled by tales of the *shee*—the faery people. I heard stories of changeling babies in cradles and missing children pulled by the wee folk into their underground kingdoms, never to be seen again.

And how I wanted to believe in those fables. Because my main concern was not the Irish Revolution, but being saddled with my baby sister, Betty, and my toddler brother, John. In the European tradition, which my small American soul didn't want to accept, the oldest girl was expected to be a caregiver.

"Take the little ones out to play," Mom would say as she helped Gran clean the house.

I came to dread those words and the sight of the wash rags. My life would have been ideal if I didn't have the plague of John and Betty hanging over me, their whines cutting into my day-dreams, their incessant demands for entertainment interrupting the read of a good book. I prayed the wee folk *would* carry them away—far away.

One day, a year after we had arrived, Mom shooed me out the door in the by now familiar fashion, Betty riding my hip and John clinging to my hand.

I remember that day in all its detail. It was a crisp June morning. White clouds chased across an unusually blue sky—and I wanted nothing more than to wander alone through knee-high primroses. But once again I found myself hampered by baby Betty and rosy-cheeked John.

My brother immediately toddled off toward the fence that surrounded the forbidden Church of Ireland graveyard. "Horsey!" he cried, spotting Mr. Riley's nag grazing under ancient elms.

"John," I yelled, tackling him in mid-stride.

"Me see horsey," he screamed, kicking at me.

Just then, I saw Betty crawl up an incline and onto the railroad tracks a good fifty feet away. She liked to skip down the line of even wooden planks, but Mom had expressly said she wasn't to go up there. I let go of John and dashed toward my sister. Straightaway, he made a dive for the churchyard.

"Oh, no you don't," I said, snatching at his arm and dragging his suddenly limp, dead weight toward Betty.

"Let go, let go!" he howled.

By the time I reached the railroad tracks, Betty had disappeared down the other side. I wrestled John over the rails and scrambled to overtake her. When I caught my sister, her new, white pinafore was streaked with mud and one stocking was torn. I'd catch hail Columbia from Mom for this. I lifted her, and tried to balance her squirming body on my hip. Betty's fist closed around a large lock of my hair, and she yanked with all her might.

"Owwww!" I dropped the nuisance, John twisted free, and both went running off.

That was it for me. "Good riddance to you," I muttered, and stalked away from them. Out of the corner of my eye, I caught movement, and turned.

Four men were running wildly across the field toward us, one some distance ahead. I recognized three British Black and Tans, and I could identify the man they were chasing. He was an officer of the Irish Republican Army. The Brits were screaming curses at their quarry, which only made him run faster. He sprinted by me, and my hair blew back from the force of the wind he created.

"Halt! Halt!" the English yelled.

I saw one raise his rifle. Another soldier pointed at us.

"Look! There are children in the way."

"So what? Bloody Irish. What's a few less in the world?" And the first soldier fired his gun. The others followed suit.

I couldn't move. The bullets whizzed by so close, I could feel the breeze from them. *Betty. John.* Betty's face peeked out from a clump of daisies. Her eyes were wide with confusion.

"Me play guns." John trotted toward the Black and Tans.

"No," I gasped, and tackled my siblings, pulling them down with me into the sheltering grass. All I wanted was to protect them. Another bullet whistled past, and I muffled a scream in Betty's silky hair. We were going to die.

"Mary?" John whimpered.

"Stay down. Stay down."

I dared a glance up. Standing twenty yards beyond me was the Irish patriot. My young mind couldn't comprehend. Why had he stopped? Why hadn't he thrown himself into the grass, too? Why wasn't he running?

His face still haunts my dreams, a blanched mask of helplessness and despair. It was as if he were saying, *Where can I go? What can I do now?*

Bam! Another shot. The wind left the young man in a loud whoosh, the strangest sound I'd ever heard. Blood spread across his shirt, and he fell. I wanted to get up and help him but the English were coming. I had to keep my brother and sister hidden or they would kill us, too. I ducked down and scrunched us even deeper into the grass. Hours seemed to creep by, although I'm sure it was mere minutes until all was silent.

"Now," I whispered, tugging John and Betty toward the fence that cut us off from home. For once in their lives, they listened. We crawled, afraid to stand, afraid we'd be shot.

I looked around once when we got to the rock wall. Two Black and Tans were dragging the patriot out of the field by his arms. The other carried the guns. "Quick," I panted, pushing on Betty's bottom until she dropped to the other side. In a spurt of strength I didn't know I possessed, I lifted John across. Once clear of the killing field, we flew home.

All of us stopped at Gran's front door, gasping and sobbing. Betty squeezed my finger until the tip was red, and John clung to my waist, his face buried under my arm.

In the seconds it took to control myself, I had time to think. Ireland had almost claimed my brother and sister, as I had so often wished. As the realization hit me, I knew my past irritations, my former inconveniences, were petty and stupid. Betty and John were the living, precious reality, a vital part of me, and I loved them.

The violence in Ireland so many years ago almost claimed our lives. We were innocent bystanders in a situation we didn't understand and didn't create. Today in the news I read of children caught in gang shoot-outs, killed in the crossfire. I know their fear and their family's sadness. The setting might be a graffiti-defaced corner in a trash-strewn city, not a sunny meadow, but the result is the same. My initiation into these truths and the immutable bond of family came in that summer field of primroses, so long ago.

—————⟶⟶⟶•⟵⟵⟵—————

The Republic of Ireland won its independence in 1921, and Mary's family returned to the States shortly after. John died ten years ago, but the two sisters still remain dear friends.

Olympic Spirit

By Mary Pesaresi, 40, writer

⳥⳥⳥⳥⳥

$\mathcal{I}$N THE EXCLUSIVE UNIVERSE OF WORLD-CLASS SWIMMERS, Mark Henderson is renowned—four-time U.S. champion; double gold medalist in the 1995 Pan American Games; member of the 1996 U.S. Olympic Team—to cite a mere sampling of his accomplishments. Page through the premier issue of *Cosmopolitan All About Men, Hunks in Trunks,* and you can't miss his blond good looks and million-watt smile.

After he qualified for the Olympics, he pulled from his swim trunks a lucky penny that his second-grade teacher had given to him. *USA Today* carried the story around the country. Even the Internet features his picture and stats.

To the world, Mark Henderson is a superb athlete and a budding personality. This is exciting news for my family, but we know a different Mark. To us, he is a world-class person.

Our first glimpse of him seven years ago was of a tall young man rising above a milling, squealing bunch of five-, six-, and seven-year-old swimming hopefuls, the biggest of whom barely reached his waist. Among them were my daughters, Sara and Anne.

To a kid, they stared with frightened uncertainty from the pool—whose length appeared to stretch to the horizon—to their towering assistant coach, whose head seemed to touch the clouds. I don't know which one scared them the most.

"Who can swim a lap?" Mark asked. "Raise your hand." Not an arm went up. "Who thinks they can't make it across?" Little hands shot skyward. Mark stood in the middle of a human pincushion of fear. "That's okay. Don't worry about it. Let's have some fun."

He started gently, winning even the shyest child over to him. How? Kindness, patience, and true interest. Gradually, he introduced them to deep water.

Soon, he tied a soft rubber cord around their waists, and hauled them along as they swam. Then he stopped pulling, and before they knew it, every last one of them could make it across that pool—little kids who felt they could conquer the world because of Mark.

He was as thrilled as they were, and organized a caravan of his buddies to take the whole lot of his mini-mites to see *Honey, I Shrunk the Kids.* I have to tell you, even the bravest of us moms would have thought twice, more like three times, before we tackled such an excursion.

He didn't abandon the kids after they made the team. To him, it was not win, win, win. It was fun, fun, fun. And I, with no illusions as to my darlings' abilities, appreciated it. When all was said and done, Mark wanted them to love swimming, and they did.

Now these were children, not angels, and they could be mean as hornets to each other. That didn't fluster Mark, but he didn't allow it, either.

When kids were teasing Brian because he turned blue in the water, Mark told him that when he was little, his nickname was

Grape Ape because he was always purple after swimming. "I'm going to Atlanta," he gasped after his Olympic trials race this spring. And, yep, his lips were blue.

When my daughter Sara walked away from a fellow swimmer who taunted her for finishing in second place, Mark took note. At the end of the summer, he gave her the good sportsmanship award, and made her feel as if it was a more important trophy than any other.

→→→•←←←

The second season Mark coached, he started the summer with a picnic in the park for the kids on the team. This had never been done before. No other coach wanted to bother. As the team's social chairman, I helped him organize it. This time, it wasn't the kids who were the problem. Now he had to put up with complaints from the parents!

"Nobody will come."

"There are bugs in the park."

"Why can't we have it here by the pool?"

"We've never done this before."

When these moms started whining, Mark was bewildered. "I don't understand," he'd ask me. "Am I doing something wrong?"

"Certainly not. It's too bad you have to learn a lesson in grown-up griping at such a young age. Some parents think you don't pay enough attention to their kid, and you pay too much to the ones who are as slow as turtles."

"But that's why they need my attention."

"Exactly. Just keep doing what you're doing. The kids love it. That's what's important."

Sixty people showed up for Mark's picnic, and we had a ball. He never once let the parents' complaints turn him from his interest in the children.

The team didn't have a winning season—our little team *never* had a winning season. But the kids didn't get down about it because Mark never did.

Four years later they still think Mark is awesome—and not because of his swimming abilities or his renown. "He liked me." "He thought I was good."

Mark gave each child he touched something that glows in them even today—self-confidence. And watching his startlingly mature wisdom has taught this parent a lesson.

He knew children become what you expect them to be. If you like them, and think they're good, they will be.

→→→ • ←←←

Mark won a gold medal and helped set a world record for the men's 4x100 meter medley relay, the last swimming event for the Centennial Olympics. This is the crowning achievement of twenty years of training, but to us, Mark has always been a champion.

Irreplaceable

By Kenneth Smith, 36, real estate developer

✦✦✦✦✦

ONE OF MY MOTHER'S FAVORITE SAYINGS WHEN I WAS A BOY was, "If my father said 'Jump,' we children would ask, 'How high?' and 'When should we come down?'" The implicit lesson was that we were to react to her in the same manner she had reacted to *her* father.

My father was a professor at the state university. Raising a large family on a professor's salary was an art in itself, but my mother did an incredible job of making us comfortable. We lived in a large home, which she always kept finger-test clean and artfully furnished with pieces she'd pick up from thrift stores and refinish. The house had a formal living room that was a half-flight of stairs above our front entry way. Between these two areas was an expanse of open bookcase where my mother displayed her finest treasures.

One afternoon when I was twelve, I was alone and doing something that I knew was expressly forbidden—playing ball in the sacrosanct living room area. But I was being extra careful about where it bounced, and I was sure that nothing bad was going to happen. Then the ball hit an uneven spot in the rug and ricocheted upward. With uncanny precision it flew straight through one of the openings in the bookcase, taking with it my mother's most cherished possession—one of two matching antique vases imported from England that she'd inherited from her mother.

Like an Olympic diver, the vase turned over in the air three times before crashing onto the tiled entryway floor below. I watched the delicate china fragment into what seemed to me a thousand pieces. I knew it was hopeless to try to glue the heirloom back together, so I cleaned up the mess, hid the shattered shards in my bedroom, and sat on the bottom stair waiting in awful anticipation for mother to come home.

"What are you doing, son?" she asked as she came in the front door an hour later. I jumped up to face her but couldn't get the words out. "Is something the matter, Kenny?"

At this question all my practiced bravery broke down. I stood in front of her, bawling like the child I was, trying to get out what had happened. My mother's eyes strayed upward to the empty place on the bookshelf. Then, slowly, they traveled to where its match still stood in solitary splendor. Finally, they came back to rest on my pinched face.

My mother dropped her purse on the entry table. "Come here, son," she said. I stumbled forward and she gathered me into her arms. She held me close, my head against her chest, and stroked my hair. This was a totally unexpected response and I sobbed even harder. "Sssshh, ssshhh," my mother soothed.

When I'd calmed down, she led me back to the bottom stair and sat me down beside her. "I want to tell you something very important, son," she began. "And I want you to listen and remember. Nothing, no object in this house, including mother's vase, is as important to me as the people who live here. Everything in this house is replaceable, Kenny. Everything, that is, but our family. You are all that really matters. You are irreplaceable."

→→→•←←←

My wife and I are nearing the end of the impossible task of restoring a classic Victorian home built in 1916, while simultaneously raising three rambunctious youngsters. When I am tempted to explode at my boys for black thumbprints on a newly painted wall, or for innocently putting a ding in the just-refinished cherrywood trim, the wisdom of my mother comes to mind. Everything in our home is replaceable, with the exception of the years my boys spend growing up there.

→→→•←←←

The remodeling was finished in the summer of 1996. Kenneth is happy to report that husband, wife, children, and house are all intact and doing well.

The End of the Rainbow

By Sara Pesaresi, 14

❦

*W*HEN I WAS TWELVE, GRANDMA CALLED MY SISTER, ANNE, and me "How would you girls and your mom like to see Ireland? Grandpa and I want to take you this summer. I want you to know and love the land where my parents came from."

"Yes! Yes!" we answered, excited at the prospect but not surprised. My grandparents were always giving us wonderful treats, and I'm ashamed to admit that I'd come to expect them.

One month later we were in Ireland. I didn't know so many types of green existed in this world until I saw its meadows and mountains. We explored old castles, and felt our eyes sting from the smoke of peat fires burning in Connemara cottages.

Best of all, we spent hours searching for family and Grandma's childhood memories. Grandma's mother was from Drogheda, a medieval city steeped in history, and it was one of our main destinations.

We were twenty miles from town, driving in the soft drizzle and muted sunshine of an Irish summer day, when a rainbow appeared. The end of it touched down in the meadow to our right, tinting the sheep with yellow, pink, and blue. It was as lovely a sight as any Ireland had yet offered, and none of us had ever seen the rainbow's end.

We expected it to be gone as quickly as it came, but it lingered, leading us on for a full hour, sometimes making the road a translucent kaleidoscope, or melting the gray-green meadows into watercolor pastorals.

It seemed a bridge—one that beckoned yet could not be crossed—to another time, another place. "Grandma," I said, "it's your mother's spirit welcoming you home."

Grandma didn't laugh at my thoughts. "I think you're right, Sara. But I think she's welcoming all of us."

My mom was uncharacteristically quiet in the front passenger seat. I leaned forward and tapped her on the shoulder. "Tell me about your grandmother, Mom."

"I didn't know her. She died before I was born."

"Oh, yeah. Sorry, Mom, I'd forgotten." In fact, I'd never thought about it before. How horrible. What a terrible gap in Mom's life never to have known her grandmother.

Sitting so close to Grandma, I could smell roses, the fragrance that seemed to always hover around her like a phantom. I watched her blue eyes follow the rainbow that showed us the way to her mother's birthplace.

What if I had never known her? Everything I did was of interest to Grandma. When Anne and I received our report cards, her house was our first stop after school. She'd have the table set with pretty dishes and special cakes, and she and Grandpa would count our A's over and over, telling us how proud they were. What if she'd never been there to walk with me along the beach in search of shells? And what about the plays I would have missed, and the museums to which she loved to take me?

What would my life be if I had missed moments like this?

"Look, Sara," Grandma whispered as if her voice might break the spell of the rainbow. "There's Drogheda." In the distance, sunlight turned the medieval spires of the city into gold, and our rainbow disappeared as if its mission were finished.

Maybe the rainbow bridge was my great-grandmother reaching out to us. But maybe it was a bridge to understanding my own heart. Whatever it was, it gave me a gift of insight.

All my life, I'd expected Grandma and Grandpa to be there. Now I knew how incredibly lucky I was that God had granted me their presence in my life. If I have never said it before, I want to say it now. Thank you, Grandma and Grandpa. I love you, too, always and forever.

→→→• ←←←

Sara had to move away from her grandparents last year, yet distance cannot dim her love for them or their avid interest in her.

Beyond the Silence

As told to and written by Michael Ian Harr, 28, writer

O<small>N A</small> F<small>RIDAY</small> <small>EVENING IN</small> M<small>AY</small> 1992, <small>AFTER TWENTY YEARS</small> of separation, my father called.

"Hi, kid," he said in a sort of West Coast accent, as close as any native New Yorker can get. "I'm in town on business and I have the day free tomorrow. How would you like to do something?"

Time suddenly dissolved, and I was back in my five-year-old mind. "Where's Dad going?" I asked Mom.

"We're getting divorced," she said, standing beside his car with a tissue in hand.

I watched Dad drive out to the street and disappear over the hill, wondering why he never looked back at me. A year later he met a young woman. They soon married, moved to California, and started a family of their own. Thereafter I saw him at weddings and funerals.

"Well, what do you say?" he asked through the phone.

I didn't know what to say; I'd experienced so much anger and so much sadness. "How about a hike in the Appalachian mountains?" I finally answered.

"That sounds like a great idea!"

I agreed to meet him in the lobby of his hotel, the Newark Marriot, at nine the following morning.

→→→•←←←

As I drove to Newark, I felt as if I were edging closer, inch by inch, to a great, dark void. *Thomas, everything is going to be okay,* I told myself, but I still wanted to turn the car around and drive anywhere but to see my father.

Once in the lobby, I called up to his room. "Hello?"

"Yeah?" The voice on the other end sounded cold, and for a moment I thought this was all a bad dream.

"It's Thomas."

"Oh. Thomas," he said with more enthusiasm. "I have to take a quick shower. How about I meet you down there in ten minutes?"

A pang of loss slapped my face: *Why doesn't he invite me to his room?* But I knew why. I was not an intimate part of his life. *Why am I doing this?*

I waited by the bank of elevators. Twelve minutes later, two metal doors opened and revealed my father. He looked older than I remembered, and I realized I was much older than I felt.

"Oh, there you are," he said. "Thought I was going to have to look for you." He looked me over, first at my size, then the shadow of a shaved beard, and lastly my eyes. His smile blossomed and he appeared wonderstruck. I, too, saw our resemblance.

"How ya doin', Thomas?" He reached out and gripped me in a tight hug.

This outburst of affection after so many years of coldness felt inappropriate.

"Are you hungry?" he asked.

"Sure, I suppose so."

"They make a pretty good breakfast in the restaurant. Besides, they gave me two meal vouchers. I might as well use them."

—→→→•◄◄◄—

"I've been in therapy," I said, as we ate.

"Hey, get that waitress for me, would you?" he interrupted. "They gotta make another pot of coffee. This one's had it."

I waited fifteen minutes. "You know, Dad, I suffered a real loss without you."

He looked up from his plate, and for a brief, startling moment our eyes met, and I perceived a shattering sense of the sadness in him. I didn't know what to do but look down and let the subject sleep.

He pulled at the collar of his shirt. "Man, it's hot in here."

"Maybe we should go, Dad."

He nodded and called for the check. "So where are you taking me?" he asked cheerily once outside the hotel.

"To the Bearfort Range. It's near Bloomingdale."

—→→→•◄◄◄—

I remember the awful quietness inside the car as we got on the highway. It was worse than being alone and far worse than being with a stranger.

I turned onto the Garden State Parkway and drove North through the Oranges. By the time we reached Route 80, the silence was killing me. I wanted to say something to help my father feel more comfortable, but struggled with resentment.

Inevitably, I clung to my therapist's words. *Thomas, you're never going to get what you missed when you were a child. Your father keeps his distance, but he can't let go. He sends you a birthday card, a letter now and then. It's very, very little, but it says that he thinks about you.*

These words helped quell the paralyzing frustration in me. I wanted to have something more from this meeting, *but where should I begin?* The one place my father puts most of his energy is his career. "So how's work?" I asked.

"Work is work."

"It must be difficult in a large corporation."

"What do you mean?"

"Well, I'm in a small company and there's a lot of bureaucracy. It must be awful in a big one. I'm impressed. You're with the same place for over twenty years and still get promoted. You must be pretty smart."

He looked relieved. The nature of this relief inspired a sudden notion in me: His suffering was somehow greater than my own. I didn't know exactly where it came from, or how or why. I only knew that I felt it because it was familiar to me. The thought of this now filled the vacancy in me with something more than I ever had before: I could empathize with some part of my father.

I exited 80 onto 23 North. Urban sprawl turned into housing developments and shopping malls. Eleven miles later we reached the foothills of the Appalachian mountains.

A stretch of green hills rose before us. The air was cooler here and smelled fresh with the blooms of mountain laurel. I looked at Dad. He seemed to take it in.

As we wound up the mountain pass that led to the Bearfort Range, I began to wonder if he had regrets about choosing his second family over his first. *What is it like to give life to a child and then leave that child to grow without you? It must be difficult for him, to have his forsaken son, now twenty-five, driving him to the mountains!* Ironically, this was something I often dreamed of when I was a child, to have Dad drive *me* to the mountains.

I thought about the last time I was here with a close friend. We'd laughed and shared intimate details, but that friendship, for all it gave, could not touch the joy of having my father beside me. *And after all these years, he came, painful as it must be, he came back to me.*

I made a silent vow. I would not make my father's mistake. I would never let distance grow between my children and me. Whatever the cost, I would keep in touch.

Perhaps our meeting here in the mountains was not the perfect end to our troubles or the perfect beginning for the future. But like the earth, the seas, and civilization, it was offering us a chance to grow—together.

A smile turned the points of my cheeks red.

Dad looked over. "What are you smiling about?"

"Just smiling."

"Well, don't hide it!" he laughed. "That's a terrific smile!"

->>>-•-<<<-

That hike was the beginning of a friendship. Thomas and his father exchange letters now at least once a week, using e-mail. And while his twenty-year loss still plays out in his life, Thomas is thankful to have his father in his adult world.

Milestones

'Tis in truth not the
days nor the years, but
the moments that mark
our passage through life.

—Anonymous

A Plateful of
Mortal Sins

From Mary Beth, between 30 and death, former Catholic schoolgirl

❦

$\mathscr{I}$ WAS IN SECOND GRADE IN THE EARLY 1960s, WHEN NUNS
were nuns and kids were scared of them. Those were the good old
days when the principal—fondly referred to as Sister Rocky
Marciano—might descend at any moment and administer "divine
justice" to some mischief-maker's backside. We all knew that if we
toed the line, we could escape the righteous wrath of The Rock.

But nothing we could do helped us avoid the cold, gray, moral
gaze of Sister Terence, the god of Class 2A—our teacher of the
Omnipotent, the link for our seven-year-old souls to an awesome
and terrible God. That's where I learned, as Elmer Davis once put
it, the first and great commandment: Don't let them scare you.

I remember the exact moment my troubles began. Up until this
I was guilty of none of the mortal sins the dread Terence had
described. I had never killed anyone; I didn't covet anybody's wife,
whatever that meant; I always ate fish (yuck!) on Fridays, and Sunday saw me in my pew at church. All in all, hell seemed a remote
possibility, and I felt pretty darn good about it. But the helping of
mortal sins Sister was dishing up for us today was different.

"If you touch certain parts of your body, it is a mortal sin of impurity," she pronounced.

Huh? I thought, as I sat bolt upright. Wait a minute here, I touched every part of my body—heck, I *scrubbed* every part of my body—*every night*. I took baths. And now this black-and-white messenger from heaven had told me a mortal sin was involved.

Sister Terence's pasty countenance swiveled in my direction. "You must remember this when you make your First Confession next month."

I was stunned. A tad more information was required here: namely, *what parts?* I mean, she was talking mortal sin. Unlike venial sin (a lesser offense), if you have one of these doozies in God's Big Book when you die, you get kicked down to you-know-where. And I had it on the best authority—my brother Mike—that hell was worse than taking piano lessons from Sister Carlissa.

I glanced at the other second-graders, all slightly sick-looking in forest green uniforms. Brian Palank lobbed a spitball at Delores Filipelli. George Holt picked his nose. Little Zabowski, condemned by his last name to forever occupy the last desk in the last row, played with his eye patch and drooled—his normal state.

They were totally unconcerned with the massive moral issue that had been set before us. Like a bolt from the blue, the answer to this riddle hit me. Everyone else in the second grade knew *what parts*.

The error of my ways had been shown to me with horrible clarity. No more could I plead the great Catholic excuse—if you didn't know it was a sin, it wasn't. All of a sudden, to be clean of body was to be dirty of spirit.

It didn't occur to me to doubt the dread Terence's word. She was the Moses of our cinderblock Mount Sinai. And that was the end of innocence.

I tried to fake my baths, running the water until steam misted the bathroom. Mom got suspicious when my hair hung in greasy strings. She—oh, the horror of it all—she made me wash. Every night before bed she would run the bath herself, and every night I'd choke on my prayers.

"If I die before I wake, I pray my Lord my soul to take." Yeah! Fat chance. By my best estimate, I had ten mortal sins of impurity on my soul, and the tally would climb higher before First Confession. I felt sick.

→→→•←←←

The confessional was dark, and I could see the priest leaning against the little window of mesh that separated us.

"Bless me, Father, for I have sinned. This is my first confession."

"Yes, child, go on."

A listing of venial sins seemed to be the best way to ease into it. "I hit my brother Jim seven times. I threw the liver from my dinner plate under my brother Mike's chair, so he'd get in trouble."

Sweat beaded on my brow. I was breathing in short pants.

"Are you finished, little girl?"

"No." *Say it, you have to say it, say it.* "I've committed . . . twenty-fivemortalsinsofimpurity." I blurted it out, hoping that it wouldn't sound so bad if I said it real fast.

"Twenty-five mortal sins of impurity?" the priest repeated in an agonizingly slow voice. "How old are you?"

"Seven."

"What did you do?"

"I—" Oh, the guilt. "I touched my body."

The priest paused. I wondered if he was shocked to silence. Then—he *yawned*. "Listen, don't worry about it. I'm sure it was a venial sin. For your penance do four Hail Marys and three Our Fathers. And send in the next kid, will ya?"

Don't worry about it? Easy for him to say. A venial sin? Ha! I was no longer so naive.

The months that followed were a tiny taste of eternal suffering.

→→→•←←←

"What's your problem, fatty?" my brother Mike asked one day as he passed my room.

"None of your beeswax, elf-ears."

"You got Twinkies. I'm gonna tell Mom."

"You do, and I'll tell her you were making funny phone calls again."

"You do, and I'll sock your face."

"Oh, yeah?" I challenged.

"Yeah!"

Mike and I were renowned for our stunning repartee.

"What's bugging you?" he demanded.

I could not stand it anymore, my guilt was overpowering me. I didn't want to go to hell. "Mike, please tell me. What parts am I not supposed to touch?"

"You nuts?"

"No. S'ster Terence told us that to touch certain parts of our bodies was a mortal sin of impurity, only she didn't tell us what parts. Please tell me."

"You scared?" he asked.

"Every time I take a bath."

"Geez." He walked into the room and plopped himself on my bed, thinking for a minute. Then he grinned. "Don't you know you don't have to believe everything the dread Terence spouts?"

"No."

"Well, you don't. I'll tell you who you can believe every time."

"Who?"

"Mom and Dad, you idgit. Mom and Dad." I swear I saw a halo circle Mike's head with those words. "Feel okay now?"

"Yeah."

"Good. If anybody gives you a hard time, you tell me. 'Cause, you know, you're not so bad—for a girl." He made a quick grab at the package on my bed. "Gimme a Twinkie."

When he left I immediately sought out my mother. In a few minutes, I sobbed the whole story into her apron. Not once did she laugh, not once did she scold. She held me, and told me that bathing was no more a mortal sin than combing my hair.

That night I said my prayers sincerely. I asked a special benediction for Mike because he opened my eyes to what should have been obvious. And to my Mom for saving me from the fiery pit of hell.

>>-•-<<

Mary Beth, a teacher herself now, has brought a wonderful understanding of children to her classroom. She knows firsthand how children can misconstrue the most innocent of remarks, and can saddle themselves with tremendous, undeserved guilt. Her goal is to build self-worth as well as knowledge in every student she teaches.

One in a Million

By Christy Deboe Hicks, 39, Director of Public Affairs,
New York University School of Education

෴

ON OCTOBER 16, 1995, AFRICAN-AMERICAN MEN FROM
all over the country gathered on the Mall in Washington, D.C., for
the Million Man March. It was a rally born in controversy because
it was promoted as a men-only event, and because it was organized
by Louis Farrakhan, the controversial head of the Nation of Islam.

But the march was bigger than one man, broader than one
ideology, and memorable for the sea of faces that came, stood, and
listened to speeches and songs from the podium. It was memorable as well for the emotional connection these men—whose
numbers were estimated from 500,000 to 1.5 million—made
with each other and the nation . . . one face, one story at a time.

My father went to the Million Man March. His was one of those
faces, one of those stories. That this seventy-year-old African-
American man boarded a subway from his middle-class home in
northwest Washington to participate in this day of atonement and
hope makes me very proud. That he felt the need to go makes me a
little sad.

I am a child of the civil rights movement. My parents believed fervently in Dr. King's dream for an integrated and fair society in which people would be judged by the "content of their character, not the color of their skin." My parents had both suffered the indignities of a segregated society that did not value them. My mother grew up in the Jim Crow South, my father in Florida and Pittsburgh. Even his experiences in the army and on his job were not colorblind, but blinded by color.

But they believed. They hoped. They prayed. And they worked to realize the dream, not for themselves, but for their children.

My father was an integral and wonderful part of my childhood. Though he was not very different from my friends' fathers, he was worlds apart from the American image of the black male. Far from absent, he was the centerpiece of the happy memories of picnics in Virginia's mountains, bus trips to Boston, excursions to Maryland's beaches, and weekends in New York City.

I learned to bowl (though not very well) with my father's instruction. I learned to love football through my father's enthusiasm for the game. Watching basketball still brings back memories of the countless trips my father made to take us to high school games. From PTA meetings, to school performances, to graduations, to the walk down the aisle on my wedding day, my father was always there. He wanted us to have it all—to experience it all.

While at American University studying international relations, my older sister wanted to make a trip to east Africa. My mother reasoned that they could not afford to pay for the trip. My father reasoned that my sister could not afford *not* to go. She went to Africa.

Syracuse University was my first choice for a college. I was accepted and given a partial scholarship, but my mother worried about the expense. They had just put one daughter through school, and I had a younger sister who would begin college the next year. My father's only thought was that I wanted to be a journalist and that this was a good path to that goal. I went to Syracuse.

My father's own childhood had been marred by the loss of his parents at a young age, but he had embraced fatherhood and family life with a fervor and skill that belied his experience. He had faith in the strength of family. He believed in the promise of America. And he hoped and he prayed that his family would one day enjoy the fruit of that promise.

We attended integrated schools and an integrated church. My parents, especially my father, encouraged and supported our cross-race friendships. They spoke passionately and constantly of the importance of not harboring prejudice, of not lowering ourselves to respond to those who spewed hate. *Rise above it, a new day is coming.* They believed. They hoped. They prayed.

My father was at Dr. King's March on Washington. He took my older sister with him. My mother stayed home with my younger sister and me, and we watched on television.

I was struck by that memory when I learned that my sister had taken my father to the march (well, actually to the subway he would ride to the event), and my mother had stayed home with my younger sister and watched on television. They believed. They hoped. They prayed.

But this time the hope was different. The three decades between my father's two journeys to the Mall had taught us much—as individuals, as a family, as a community. In many ways my father's and my mother's dreams had been realized: Their daughters are college-educated, well-read, well-traveled women with good jobs. We have been places and done things that were never available to my parents, who are also educated with advanced degrees. We have gained access; but the promise, the dream of acceptance, still eludes my family, my community, my people.

Yes, we can get some of the jobs that were previously out of our reach, but we cannot find mentors and advocates there. We can go to the restaurants, but we are still often treated with disdain. We can afford to buy designer clothes, but sometimes are viewed with suspicion when browsing in the more exclusive shops.

We have the option of living in higher-rent districts, but discover that many realtors have coded the books in ways that limit the availability of housing to us. We can make the mortgage payments on higher-end homes, but still find it difficult to qualify for loans. When we want to sell the higher-priced homes we have managed to obtain, we are told to remove pictures of ourselves and our families so that prospective white buyers will not be turned off. Acceptance—the goal that is hardly ever articulated but ever present—is elusive.

So my father went to the Million Man March. And he joined with other African-American men who were there—and women who were not—and turned inward. He had not given up the dream, but he had come to recognize the need to change the strategy. He, like other African Americans, had long ago learned that our skin of brown and beige and black would not blend easily into a melting pot, but we had hoped to fit into the mosaic that is America.

I think most of us still do. I know my father still does. Not by reaching out our hands in supplication, but by straightening our backs, holding our heads up, being proud of all the things, and there are many, that are right in our communities, and working to fix those that are wrong. A strong, proud people command respect—even if it comes grudgingly. A people who have learned to love and respect themselves often find acceptance.

My father still goes bowling and fishing, and holds season tickets for Washington Redskins games. And he is lustily mastering the fine art of being the perfect grandfather. These are, for the most part, gentle, happy times for a man who has more than earned them. But he never forgets. And never, ever gives up.

So on this day—October 16, 1995, my father joined fathers and sons from across the nation—Americans who just wanted to hold their heads high and be judged by the content of their character, not the color of their skin. And my mother stayed home with my sister and watched on television. And once again they believed. And they hoped. And they prayed.

→→→ • ←←←

Christy Deboe Hicks comes from a family of teachers who migrated from the South to settle in the Northeast in the 1940s. Their history encompasses all the changes our capital has seen since that time. Starting on Memorial Day, 1996, Christy will be gathering the stories from a clan that has seen it all. The compilation will be woven into a book about Washington, D.C., that will chronicle a past that shows the people's side of Capitol Hill.

Something in Common

From Carolyn Kimberly Hadley, 32, homemaker

✨✨✨

SOMETIMES IT TAKES SO LONG TO APPRECIATE WHAT YOU'VE GOT. There were five children in my family, and I was the second born and the oldest daughter. From the beginning I was my father's favorite. And just as surely, my interactions with my mother, Evajean, followed one of the classic mother/daughter relationships—disagreement, discord, defiance, and disdain.

As a child I was athletic and loved sports. So did my father. Evajean, on the other hand, could have cared less about somebody kicking a ball up a field or hitting one over a net.

In my teens I was the typical adolescent girl, obsessed with fashion and makeup. It was a bad day if it didn't look like I'd stepped off the cover of *Vogue*. My father, like me, loved splurging on clothes and was an impeccable dresser. "Come on, honey," he'd say in a conspiratorial whisper, lest my mother overhear. "Let's slip down to the mall and see what we can find you."

Evajean, on the other hand, was frugal. Clothes were something you covered your body with. My mother had no taste or style. How could she? She was satisfied with only half a dozen pantsuits and shirts in her wardrobe, and she was even sloppy about those.

My closet was immaculately organized. Every dress, skirt, blouse, and sweater were hung by color and season, every pair of shoes treed, labeled, and identified for either dress, casual, or sport wear. And everything was clean. I am a fanatic about cleanliness.

Evajean, on the other hand, thought nothing of not bathing until noon. She was raised in a small town in Idaho, in circumstances that weren't very good. My mother, you see, was a hick.

My dad, who was more like me personality-wise, formed an alliance with me. He liked sports and good times—so did I. He was meticulous—so was I. He was fashionable and liked to spend money—so did I. It seemed more and more that the two of us, the whole family really, would exclude my mother from our good times.

Hawaii was a prime example. We'd go to the islands for three months every summer. For my father and the rest of us children, the beach was the place to be. All day long we'd swim and surf, play volleyball, sunbathe, or sail on a catamaran.

Evajean, on the other hand, didn't particularly like the sun or the ocean. My mother's idea of a summer on the beach in Honolulu was to hide under a palm tree and read. All I ever saw her do was read. Mysteries, thrillers, cookbooks, self-help tomes—Evajean would sit serenely under a tree and read them all. No wonder we ignored her.

I took for granted the way she encouraged me. Evajean, for instance, may not have been interested in art or have any artistic taste, but because I showed an interest, she took me to galleries and applauded my art major in college.

The natural order of things to me was a mother who always held and hugged me, and told me she loved me. I didn't see the quiet support she gave my father, how she listened and contributed.

My twenties brought my marriage, a move across country to Boston, and another kind of distancing—a physical separation. Now Evajean and I only saw each other once a year.

→→→•←←←

My son was to be born in the autumn of 1987, and Evajean was beside herself with excitement. I was amazed at the animation pouring out of the phone during her now daily calls. "Kim, how do you feel today?" she'd ask for the fifth time. "Is he kicking yet? Now you must lie down and take it easy."

"Kim, your father and I have talked it over. I'm coming for the birth and I'll stay as long as you need me. I'm planning at least two weeks."

At least two weeks! What would I do with my mother for two weeks? My husband went to school all day and studied all night, so he'd be no help. We lived in what, at a stretch, you could call a studio apartment. I would be forced to interact with this woman at close quarters on a one-to-one basis. Yet some deep part inside wanted her to come.

The doctors gave me a Cesarean to bring Hadley into the world. I didn't know it was possible to survive so much pain. But the moment I saw my son, it was all worth it. When I held this tiny six-pound baby in my arms, and gazed on his little wrinkled, red face and dark fuzz of hair, I was overwhelmed with love.

Then the door to my room opened and Evajean walked in, her slightly overweight figure dressed in its familiar conservative green pantsuit. No jewelry, a smear of pale lip gloss, her short gray hair fresh cut and permed, and the square, no-nonsense glasses whose style had never changed perched as usual, just below the bridge of her nose. Her armful of gifts tumbled onto the bed, and my newborn and I were enfolded in the most gentle, loving, embrace.

In that moment I felt a connection to my mother that was older than creation, a thread of continuity passing between the generations as it had from the beginning of time—a spiritual connection to a whole, a universal family, a vital part of the order of nature.

My mother pulled back, fearful she was holding us too close.

"Don't go," I whispered. "Don't go away."

After a while she sat on the bed, and took my son. She oohed and aahed and murmured again and again, "How beautiful he is, Kim, how perfect." She was so in love with my baby that I saw my mom through totally different eyes.

It didn't matter that we had little in common. Those things I'd thought so important were trivial in the presence of this new, major bond forming between us. Nothing had changed between us except my perception of her, and suddenly I was ashamed at the inane superiority I'd nurtured over the years, felt stupid that I had ever thought this loving woman could be inferior. "I love you, Mom."

My mother turned to me, wisdom in her eyes, acceptance of how things are and had always been—no resentment, anger, or mistrust. Just an open love that flowed over my newborn son and me like a river.

"I love you too, honey."

I have three sons now, Hadley, eight, Easton, six, and Cooper, who just turned four. Evajean was with me for each of their births. Two years ago my husband and I moved to Utah. My mom and dad were so happy when we asked them to come and live nearby.

Mom is the best grandma and the kids love her so much. I am pregnant again and I wonder about the child I'm carrying. It's too early to tell if it will be another son, or perhaps this time a daughter. I'd like a daughter. I only hope if it's a girl, she doesn't make my mistakes. I hope she doesn't waste too much time learning the important lessons in life.

→→→•←←←

Carolyn Kimberly Hadley had a daughter, Sawyer, on May 27, 1996. Evajean was by her side.

Revelation

By Brian Christopher Baumann, 15

I ONCE THOUGHT THE ESSENCE OF MY PATERNAL GRANDFATHER, Charles, was his stories, particularly the tales of his exploits as a sergeant during the Normandy campaign of 1944, but I was wrong. I found that out when my family and I were with him fifty years later as he rewalked the beaches of D-Day.

At the airport before our flight, Grandpa insisted that he carry his luggage, despite my offers to help him. "If I could carry eighty pounds of equipment for miles on end back then, I think I can manage a few light suitcases now," he laughed.

The plane landed in Charles De Gaulle airport, and we found our two rental cars. Navigating around Paris was no easy chore, especially since my grandfather had to follow my dad as he weaved in and out of rush-hour traffic. Many seniors drive slowly and deliberately, but this was not the case with my grandpa on these French roads. He reverted back to his old army days, and refused to let a car break up the convoy.

We arrived at the hotel, and my grandfather, betraying no signs of sleepiness during the drive, hit the bed and was out immediately, like a soldier after a strenuous tour of duty.

The next day I witnessed one of the most emotional experiences of his life—and mine.

We had come to Omaha Beach. The old soldier had returned to the place where he had landed fifty years ago. The first thing we saw was a huge American flag flapping valiantly in the wind, and Grandpa stared at it for a long time.

"It was that symbol, and what it represents, that drove those young men into a gale of bullets in defense of freedom," he mumbled. Then he walked ahead so we wouldn't see him cry.

We followed him through a beautiful garden and there, laid out at our feet, was a huge expanse of white headstones extending in every direction as far as the eye could see—a solemn city of death, the American Cemetery.

Grandpa whispered to my sister, "Under each of these crosses and stars is a young man who never got to have grandchildren like I did, but they are all heroes." A lone tear trickled down his cheek and fell into the mud.

In a nearby chapel was a mural depicting a dead GI on Omaha Beach clutching a blood-stained flag to his chest as angels bore him away. Somehow that picture brought the carnage to life for me, and I studied it with Grandpa before he turned away and led us to an office.

Inside he found the book that documented the names of the dead. He wanted to see where a friend of his who had died on Omaha Beach on D Day was buried. I saw him cringe at the thickness of the book.

I watched Grandpa's face as he paged through the records. He had not given the sacrifice of his life, and thank God for it. But here, on the shores of Omaha, because of Grandpa's fierce desire to share with me and my sister, history was alive and breathing with the victory and cataclysm of fifty years past.

He once told me that the war had changed him. He saw his buddies willing to lay down their lives for strangers, and had witnessed the suffering of the people of France and England. He was never the same again. But never once did he mention that he was fighting alongside his friends, that he was also willing to make the ultimate sacrifice.

Right then, I knew my grandfather was a hero, too. Not just because he was a decorated soldier—which he was—but because he had set aside such bitterness as he might have been expected to feel, and had lived his life for the good. It's hard to strive for the highest, but because he does, he makes me want to try.

I looked at Omaha Beach at that moment as if I had new eyes. The ocean lapping softly against the sand at twilight was so tranquil. Seagulls squawked and frolicked in the surf. An osprey flew toward the setting sun . . . toward America. It was as though the earth had forgotten the horror here fifty years ago on the sixth of June.

But my grandfather, gazing on the murder scene of so many young soldiers, saw the vista as it had appeared to him, a boy, fifty years before. I was looking at something else—a man. In his kindness, through his love, in his example of hard work, I know that Grandpa is all that makes a man good.

"Don't ever forget, Brian," he said suddenly.

It was not a battle from World War II that I was thinking about at that moment. "I never will, Grandpa."

→→→•←←←

Brian wrote this essay for a middle-school assignment. His teacher was so moved she entered it in a contest judged by teachers, and never mentioned it to Brian. Out of thousands of entries, this essay was picked as one of the top fifteen, and Brian was named one of the most "promising young writers in the country."

Unexpected Teachers

*When one is helping
another, both are strong.*

—German proverb

Libby, the Christmas Angel

As told to Mary and Samantha

✦

*L*IBBY WASN'T TWO YEARS OLD WHEN HER PARENTS FIRST brought her to me for radiation therapy. Tiny, bald, suffering from a rare type of incurable cancer we doctors referred to as "baby killers," Libby was the sum of her suffering and no more, the poster child of all terminal infants.

She broke my heart, but as an oncologist I knew only too well that all I could do was ease the pain of her day-to-day existence. Professionalism was vital when treating a case like hers—a physician could easily be torn in two when confronted by such waste of human life. I had to close myself off to Libby and treat her with kind indifference, or so I told myself.

I am a religious man. I believe in the eternal goodness of a loving God, but I could not reconcile this tormented innocent with such an idea. Her short life would be one of ever-worsening pain that her parents would have to watch and endure. Not for them the first day of school, best friends, first crush. For them, nothing.

Why had she ever been born?

185

Libby's first series of treatments took place daily over fourteen days. She lay limp and apathetic, unresponsive to any stimulation. Her parents were silent, poker-faced, and efforts at small talk seemed ridiculous in light of their monumental distress. So I honored their quiet. Besides, it made it easier to keep my professional detachment—so I told myself.

After a few weeks, Libby's pain began to subside. Instead of flat, dull eyes, I caught fleeting glimmers of interest in their brown depths. Flashes of a sweet, mischievous personality began to emerge. My God, she even had dimples when she smiled, and how wonderful to me was that first smile.

A great weight seemed to lift from her parents, too. I won't forget my delight when I walked into my office to interrupt a wild combination of peek-a-boo and pat-a-cake, accompanied by bubbles of laughter.

Imagine, Libby laughing.

With this blossoming came another side of the child. She started to make her likes and dislikes well known to my nurses and me, and I don't know why I was surprised that her list wasn't too different from that of my own two-year-old.

"No shot," she'd cry, squirming under her mommy's arm. Then she'd contort her little body to try to hide the side of the thigh where the nurse had to poke her needle.

It became a game, with my nurse as the bad guy who gave Libby the shot and me as the good guy who saved her from the mean lady. My poor nurse had the patience of Mother Theresa and played the role without protest, and I was Libby's savior—so I told myself.

The radiation equipment in my office looks like something out of *Star Wars,* but Libby's favorite treat became "riding the table."

The table moves up, down, and sideways to deliver the pinpoints of radiation exactly where needed. But for this child who would never see Disneyland, we turned our machine into a toddler thrill ride.

My staff loved Libby's visits. They began to vie with each other to see who would bring the best balloons, lollipops, or stuffed animal to give her that day. They'd spend inordinate amounts of time fussing over her, their faces soft with silly smiles. I understood now why her parents felt that Libby had enriched their lives immeasurably. She certainly enriched ours.

Six months into Libby's therapy, we could do no more. On the last day, we all took turns saying good-bye and could barely hide our tears when she put her arms around each of our necks and pressed her lips against each of our cheeks. At that moment I would have sold my soul to give this child the one gift beyond my reach—her life.

The dreaded phone call came too soon. Libby had died at 3:06 on a Thursday morning. The clinic was full of openly crying technicians, nurses, and physicists. And it was not the waste of Libby's existence for which they mourned. It was for the child herself—that so vital, loving, cranky, sweet self.

My wife and I attended her funeral, sadly near Christmas, and afterward we bought a waxen angel clothed in crimson velvet to remind us always of the newest, littlest angel in heaven.

Had I truly wondered why she had ever been born? Had I really questioned the existence of a good, loving God? Libby had brightened every life she touched, every one of us.

It has been thirteen years since Libby passed away. Every year, my family carefully unwraps Libby the Angel from her tissue, and one of my children has the honor of placing her namesake on top of our Christmas tree. Every year they beg me to tell them of Libby the person.

Through her story they have learned that life, no matter how short, is the most precious of God's gifts. And as long as her tale is told, Libby, in a greater sense, will live forever—in the hearts of my wife and children, and always in my own.

※ ·

In his years of practice, this doctor has had to treat too many Libbys. But he gives thanks to the tiny child for allowing him to see all his patients as precious individuals, and to God for allowing him to help cure many of them.

The Other Side of Fifteen

From Pamela Wiss, 44, advertising account executive

To UNDERSTAND THIS STORY YOU NEED TO KNOW ABOUT the nuns of Holy Trinity, where my son, Todd, attended grade school. These sisters are not your modern, habit-less nuns with social consciences and careers to match. They are great, no-nonsense teachers, which is exactly why my son declared war on them. As some wise person once said, there's nothing wrong with kids that reasoning with them won't aggravate.

You see, Todd liked to negotiate, but the sisters' idea of bargaining was to state what was expected, then demand it, and grade accordingly. Todd saw that as absurd, and tried during his years at Holy Trinity to make them see reason—his way. He failed, and was forced to toe an unwilling, grumbling line. "They'll get theirs," he'd mumble on occasion, shaking a fist at the bricks and mortar he called his prison.

It had been four years since Todd escaped the nuns' clutches, but up to that day, July 11, 1993, an armistice had never been proclaimed.

189

July 11 was a day that burst the thermostat at a soul-searing 108 degrees. That afternoon Todd and I, and a car full of groceries, were riding past the convent where the nuns live. We drove in silence. As always, Todd was staring out of the window, wrapped in his own world, ignoring me—his usual, scintillating teenage company.

"I smell smoke," he said, suddenly coming to life.

I ignored him. Payback time.

"Mom, I smell smoke."

I drew in a deep breath, and darned if I didn't pick up a whiff of it, too.

Todd leaned forward and squinted out of the windshield. "Mom, the convent's on fire."

I slowed down and craned to see. Sure enough, smoke rose in thick, black billows from the roof of the building. "Oh, isn't that a shame," I said, not thinking. "I hope no one's been hurt."

"Mom. *Duh!*" Todd said. "Where are the fire trucks?"

I stopped the car. "Huh?" I grunted. I clung to the steering wheel, paralyzed by indecision.

Todd grabbed the car phone and dialed 911. "There's a fire. In the nuns' house on 35th Street," he yelled to the operator. "Has anyone called it in? No? Well I suggest you get your butts over to 35th, like now." He jammed the phone back in its cradle.

We sat in the car and watched as flames shot from the roof of the convent. Why hadn't any nuns come out yet? This was getting scary.

"Where are they?" Todd demanded.

"The fire trucks should have been here," I said lamely.

He gave me his best "get real" look. "No duh." My vision turned red. "No duh" to a parent is like fingernails scraping a blackboard. Overpowering irritation reduced me to a useless, quivering mass.

But Todd wasn't useless. He hesitated for half a second then jumped out of the car. "Sister Regina," I heard him mutter. For an instant, I detected glee. I knew what he was thinking as well as I knew my own name: *Let them burn.*

Then the car door slammed shut. "Run to the fire station on Volta Street," my son yelled as he loped away. "I'm going to get the nuns out."

What? He was going to get the nuns? "Todd, come back. Don't you go in that building. Tooooddd!"

I scrambled out of the car and followed. My son's roar pulled me up short. "Mom, get back in the car, block the street and stop the traffic." The wail of sirens answered my prayers. "Let the fire trucks through."

That sounded logical, so I did it.

And there I stood, the quintessential traffic cop—sweat drenched, sunburned, and irritated. And where was Todd? When a fireman thought to relieve me of my duty, I rushed in search of my son.

I saw him, hands in his pockets, strolling toward a soda machine as if he didn't have a care in the world. He reached it before I did, and proceeded to feed coin after coin into the slot.

"What happened to you?" I demanded.

Todd calmly gathered up an armful of sodas. "Where?"

"For God's sake, at the convent. Remember that? 'I, Todd, am going to save the nuns?'"

A last Coke rolled out of the machine. "Nothing."

My son scooped the ice cold cans to his chest and sprinted past me. That did it. I ran after him to give him a piece of my fried mind, then stopped.

Todd had reached a group of disheveled nuns, miserable in their smothering habits. I watched in awe as he handed the blessed Coca-Colas to each one of them in turn. They swarmed around him, gazing up at my tall boy in gratitude.

And he was *talking* to them. Not one-word answers delivered in a bored monotone, but complete sentences. He was being—dare I say?—polite.

As I approached I saw Sister Regina, Todd's worst nemesis, shake her head as if bewildered. "I always used to complain about you, and now . . ." She waved toward the smoldering building. "God bless you."

"It's okay, S'ster," he mumbled. "Wasn't nothing."

"Anything," Sister Regina corrected. "It wasn't anything."

Todd just grinned, and she smiled back.

The rest of the afternoon is a blur of motion and emotion. In spite of my son's secret vow never to communicate with his mother, I found out what happened. Todd's ear-splitting shouts had been enough to alert the nuns before the fire could be fatal. As soon as he figured the sisters were safe, he'd taken himself to the opposite end of 35th and proceeded to make sure the fire trucks could get through. Not bad for a fifteen-year-old.

I kept glancing at Todd as we drove home. Typically, his face was turned to the window. He had resumed that tired-of-it-all adolescent slouch. But it didn't fool me anymore. I'd seen the other side of fifteen, and it bodes well for the years to come. I was so proud, I felt I would burst. I love him, my brave, fast-thinking son.

→→→• ←←←

The convent that burned on July 11, 1993, was part of the Georgetown Visitation Girls' Preparatory School. The nuns of Holy Trinity share the convent with the sisters of the Visitation. Todd was interviewed by local news stations, and his proud parents still have the videotape.

Mustafa

From Joe Paul, 44, hotel marketing executive

BOOM!

It sounded like The Bomb, and I would have looked for the tell-tale mushroom cloud except I was in a life-and-death fight with my Toyota. The steering wheel went out of control, and I felt the car careen across three lanes of icy, bumper-to-bumper highway before finally coming to rest on the left shoulder.

It took a minute for my breath to return. I was alive, but my situation couldn't have been worse. Blowout on the D.C. Beltway. At rush hour, of course. In freezing rain, naturally.

It was no use trying to change the tire. In the dark I'd be smashed to bits. And I couldn't attempt to cross four lanes of wild-eyed pedestrian predators. I'd be horsemeat.

Smashed to bits or horsemeat was not the way I wanted to meet eternity.

As I clicked on the emergency lights, melodrama took possession of my soul. In a great wave of self-pity, I pictured the scene a couple days hence.

My little family—draped in black—would throw themselves on my coffin in an agony of good-byes. My wife would squirm under

194

the unbearable guilt of having put the kibosh on my planned purchase of a forty-six-inch, 3-zillion channel super TV. Oh, how she'd regret it when they laid my cold, lifeless body at her feet.

So I waited for help, nursing morbid thoughts, hoping a state trooper might have left the snug confines of Dunkin' Donuts to actually brave the highway. What an optimist I was. An hour passed and nothing. Nobody. An hour and a half crawled by. I resigned myself to sleeping in the back seat until daylight.

Suddenly, out of the night, a brand-new gold Pontiac taxicab pulled onto the shoulder in front of me. Oh, wonderful. I had exactly two bucks in my pocket, and cabbies aren't known for their readiness to accept personal checks.

I turned my collar high, leaned into the sleet, and ran to the taxi. The window rolled down, and a very friendly face surrounded by a halo of dreadlocks smiled at me. "Get in," he invited, "I'll get you to a gas station."

"I don't have any cash."

"No worries. Get in, my friend. Mustafa is my name."

What a nice voice he had, full of good humor, undulating with the musical accents of the Caribbean. Just the sound of his voice seemed to transport me to sunny climes. As I slid into the passenger seat, I found myself wondering if all angels sported dreadlocks, or just a select few.

The inside of Mustafa's cab was spotless, redolent of new car smell. I held out my hand, and Mustafa grasped it. How good his warm hand felt against my freezing one.

"I'm Joe."

"Let's get you some help, Joe."

Mustafa eased his cab onto the blacktop, and we were caught in the infamous D.C. traffic. I knew for sure Mustafa was a heavenly visitor when none of it perturbed him. He even gave a friendly wave to a wild man who flipped us the bird as he cut in front of us.

I felt compelled to protect this kind man. "You know, Mustafa, that wasn't a greeting."

"Sure it was," he laughed. "That guy was telling me where to get off!"

Mustafa, I realized, *was* good-hearted, but he was not naive.

We pulled into a gas station. "I'm closing up," the mechanic snapped. "All we have is gas."

I'll gas you, I thought.

"You're getting wet out here," Mustafa said, cutting through my anger. Smiling, he led us into the station's tiny office.

For once I managed to keep my abrasive mouth shut and listen, and Mustafa easily and effortlessly persuaded the mechanic to unlock the tow truck and venture into the vengeful night to bring back my car.

"That's seventy bucks," the mechanic said.

I pulled out my wallet and exhibited several different credit cards.

"Cash."

"I don't have—" I felt a hand on my arm. Mustafa winked at me and pulled his billfold from his back pocket.

"Twenty, forty, sixty, and ten makes it seventy," he counted. "Now, Rick, try to make it quick if you can, please. Joe has a wife and kids worrying about him."

"You bet I will," Rick agreed, eager to please his new friend.

How did Mustafa know this guy's name? Then I spotted it on his pocket flap, as big as day. RICK. It would never occur to me to call him by name. How thoughtless of me.

I couldn't help thinking how different Rick's reaction was to me versus Mustafa. Mustafa brought out the best in people. How did he do that? Certainly his kindness played a large role in it. But I think it went beyond that. Mustafa had genuine consideration for other people. It was so palpable, it almost glowed around him.

I couldn't impose on this man anymore. As fast as I could, I scribbled a personal check, making it out for fifty dollars extra to cover Mustafa's time. "Thank you for everything, Mustafa. Please don't let me keep you any longer."

"No. No. You're not keeping me from a thing. My wife lives in St. Lucia. She won't set foot here in the wintertime, so after work, my time's my own."

He ignored the check I held. Finally, I grabbed his hand, and pressed it into his palm. "Promise me you'll cash this."

"No worries, Joe. I promise I'll cash it."

Mustafa and I talked of St. Lucia and the D.C. cab business and my family—everything under the sun—until Rick returned with my car. Once again, I held out my hand to say good-bye.

"No, Joe." Mustafa opened my trunk and took out my spare tire.

"Let me help you change that," Rick exclaimed. "We've got to get this man home to his wife and kids."

As I pulled away from the garage, Mustafa and Rick stood together waving at me. I could almost imagine my Caribbean friend inviting the mechanic for a cup of coffee and felt left out.

When I finally arrived home, my wife was as sick with worry as my imagination could have made her. When she heard the story of Mustafa, she sat down and wrote a thank you. Both my daughters did the same. Mustafa reigned as a hero in the Paul household.

→→➤ • ⬅←←

I hate to admit it, but the glow of my rescue faded quickly in my daily grind. It might have faded permanently into nothing more than a "do you believe?" story told around the kitchen table.

Except for Mustafa.

Two days after my rescue, my wife silently handed me a letter that had arrived that afternoon. When I opened the envelope, out fell fifty bucks.

"Joe, I don't want your money," Mustafa wrote. "Once someone helped me, and all he asked was that I give aid to others who might be in need. That is what I want from you, my friend. Help others. Think of it like a snowball of kindness that grows and grows from one person to the next. Maybe this snowball will grow so big, it will finally cover the earth. Your friend, Mustafa."

I don't know if I can live up to my friend's ideal, but I do know I can try. I'm a hopeless mechanic, but if I see someone broken down on the road, I stop to see what I can do. If we hear of someone in trouble through work or church, we try to help. I pray Mustafa's vision of the world can come true, and that we will all strive to change it, one kindness at a time.

→→➤ • ⬅←←

Joe Paul and his family moved to Atlanta shortly after this incident, and Mustafa must have moved also, because any further attempt at communication resulted in cards stamped "Return to sender. Addressee unknown." Sometimes Joe wonders if Mustafa was a real angel in dreadlocks, after all.

Sittie's Hands

By L. M. Azar, 40, poet

Ꮭ

BREAD-BAKING LESSONS STARTED AROUND 5 A.M. ON SATURDAY morning in the dimly lit, dank basement of Grandmother Ruth's house. I called her Sittie, "grandmother" in Arabic. Before we could begin, we'd wash down the oil-clothed table, on top of which were placed the immense stoneware bowls, tattered cotton cloths, and the tenderly worn wooden pallets used to pull the Syrian bread out of the oven. Then Sittie would gather the ingredients.

On this particular day, I was completely entranced by my grandmother's smooth, strong hands as they measured, stirred, and poured. Her right hand, which kneaded and worked the dough to perfection, was delicately embossed on the back with a feminine floral design symbolic of the universe—a mandala. As I watched the dance of her painted hands, my thoughts drifted to her small village of Bloudan, outside of Damascus, in Syria, and I recalled the story of her tattooed hand.

→→→• ←←←

Ruth, the youngest of ten and the adoration of the family, was blessed with a childhood made carefree by so many siblings to love and watch over her. She played with her pet lamb and gathered ripened olives, fallen from the trees.

When she was seven, the gypsies came to the village. The children came to take her to their encampment to play. Before following them, the little girl looked to her mother for approval. "Go, Ruth," her mother said. "Your sisters are there before you."

The child was taken by surprise when the gypsy children sneaked up behind her and grabbed her hands and feet. "No!" she cried, struggling desperately. They forced the needle into the thin flesh of her right hand and injected the blue dye. The combination of the pain and terror caused Ruth to lose consciousness. When she awoke, her mother was holding her in her arms, wiping her tears with a cool cloth, "Now, my Ruth, you are protected from the evil eye, as are all your sisters."

→→→• ←←←

"Linda," Sittie said, "come back to me."

The gypsy camp disappeared and my grandmother, elbow deep in flour, came into focus.

"Your mind is wandering, I don't think you heard anything I said. Show me what you learned, honey."

I took the ball and flattened it as she had taught me. Then, with great trepidation, I attempted to move it back and forth on my arms, as I had earlier practiced with towels. The wonderful flowing movements that I had seen her demonstrate were not easily grasped. I giggled nervously as the dough fell to the ground or stuck to my arms, requiring another sprinkling of flour.

After a few weak attempts at mastering the art, I was allowed to observe as Sittie baked the bread. My daydreaming mind drifted back to the old country. . . .

→→→ • ←←←

Ruth was never quite the same carefree little girl after her encounter with the gypsies. She became cautious of strangers and had lost the innocence that had once been hers. She carried her scar with shame, hiding her right hand whenever possible, and wasn't consoled that all her sisters had been branded with the same mark.

"Someday you might be separated from your sisters, Ruth," her mother told her, "but you will always have this brand in common."

With the passing of time her family dispersed and her favorite older sister, Mary, moved to the United States. It wasn't until many years later, when Ruth was eighteen, that she received word that Mary was quite ill and needed her help to care for her four children. She arrived on Ellis Island after a long, harrowing trip across the ocean. Her cousins were there to meet her and take her back to Indiana, where Mary lived.

Mary looked much smaller than Ruth had remembered, withered with the pain of the cancer in her body. The children watched Ruth as she bathed and comforted their mother, massaging her tired body with salves and oils. In the evenings Ruth's nieces and nephews held her hands and caressed the tattoo that had caused

Ruth such grief. They loved so dearly their mother's hand, which bore the same marking. The children hugged her and proclaimed their adoration for Ruth and her healing hands.

Ruth's shame was lifted from her shoulders then, her scar no longer visible to her own eyes. She was proud to carry the same emblem as her beloved sister.

After Mary died, the children begged for Ruth to stay. She had grown to love these children more than her own happiness, so she agreed to marry their father, Abraham, a gentleman many years her senior. Ruth later bore two more sons with Abraham, but she never showed favoritism for her own children. All six were her life.

→→➤ • ◄←←

Sittie had taken the bread from the oven. "Now Linda," she said, "you must always let the bread get a nice golden color like this before you remove it from the oven."

Again I couldn't concentrate on the baking lesson because I was so fascinated by the blue mandala. How I admired Sittie. She had been able to rise above her own shame to acceptance. My thoughts wandered to my own struggle with shame and self-consciousness, and I recalled how Sittie helped me through it.

→→➤ • ◄←←

I was thirteen years old and disliked my chubby legs, unruly hair, and whatever else I could find to despise about myself. My first coed dance was approaching and I had nothing to wear, so I decided to make a party dress myself. The result pleasing, I awaited my grand debut in a creation of my own making.

I arrived at the dance with flowers in my hair, proud of my flamingo pink dress. The Rolling Stones pounded their rhythm into our young bodies and I found myself swinging arms, stomping feet, and letting go as I had never done before.

Halfway through the evening I felt a small hole in the seam beneath my arm. The opening expanded and grew, and to the wail of Mick Jagger's "Satisfaction," I felt my dress slip away. I escaped the dance and fled like a wounded animal. I ran into the house, ashamed beyond words, and Sittie immediately made me a cup of tea, gathered me in her arms, and reassured me that I was the prettiest and most original girl at the dance. I laughed as she shared stories of embarrassing episodes from her own youth, and most importantly the wonderful story of the tattooed hand and her rise above the shame of it.

Sittie handed me the thread and needle, and between the two of us we repaired my dress. Then she quickly pressed it as I washed my face and placed a fresh flower in my hair. As we hugged good-bye, we both knew that something very special had occurred that evening. I had overcome adversity with Sittie's help and felt much stronger for it.

→→➤ • ◄←←

The nurturing aroma of bread as it baked awakened my senses, and again I returned to the present. Sittie smiled and hugged me, "Oh, my Linda, how can I ever teach you to bake bread if you don't keep your mind from drifting?"

"But I do learn from you, Sittie," I replied.

"Yes, you wander the heavens when I want you to come down to earth."

I laughed to hide the fact that I didn't know how to articulate my thoughts to Sittie. So deeply ingrained in my soul were the lessons I learned through her actions and her words. She taught me to turn shame into triumph and to accept myself.

I snuggled against her full breast, tranquility surrounding me. My body felt so secure and content in her embrace. The serenity we shared with one another, grandmother and granddaughter, is forever embossed in my memory.

→→→ • ←←←

Sittie passed away on January 28, 1982. She left Linda a photograph of her hands with the beautiful blue mandala. It is one of Linda's most prized possessions.

Intangible Rewards

From Karen Graf, 38, homemaker, and Alicia Graf, 11

✦✦✦✦✦

KAREN: OUR VENTURE BEGAN WHEN MY DAUGHTER ALICIA, ten years old at the time, saw an article in the paper about "companion dogs." It will end tomorrow when we say good-bye to Kulus, our beloved yellow Lab–golden retriever mix puppy. He is going to New York to become a service dog for a physically impaired person.

Two years ago our old dog was put to sleep after fifteen faithful years of friendship. The whole family was devastated. My husband, Bob, refused even to consider getting another dog: "I never want to endure this kind of loss again."

All my pleading couldn't convince him that fifteen years of fun, companionship, loyalty, and love were worth the pain we all suffered. Probably because I wasn't sure myself.

But Alicia felt differently. To her, a house was not a home without a dog. We thought we'd give her a bit of time to get over it, but four months later she was still adamant. She was even able to cut through Bob's grief, and slowly he began to accept the idea of a new pet.

We rescued our golden retriever, Watson, from an abusive home. Alicia loved her new dog, but she missed having a puppy. Then she heard about Canine Companions.

Canine Companions raises puppies until they can be trained for use by the physically challenged. Some become helpers for the hearing-impaired, others are companions for the wheelchair-bound.

Bob and I were apprehensive. The family would have to keep the pup for twelve to eighteen months. That's a long time to bond with an animal, and I didn't know how Alicia and her older brother Lucas would react when it came time to give it up.

My husband and I have always believed that community work is part of life, and I didn't want to dismiss Alicia's idea out of hand, but Bob would have nothing to do with the plan.

"Please, Dad, it's just for a short time," Alicia begged.

"Absolutely not," he said time and again.

Canine Companions invited us to some of their functions. We went and got to see folks with their puppies, and meet the people who depended on the dogs who graduate.

It was wonderful to see such human/canine partnerships that embraced not only love, but mutual need. It brought to vivid life how much these dogs could change the existence of people who crave independence as much as any of us. What a gift to give. My husband's eyes were shining after he'd met some of the canines and their people.

"Yes," he said to Alicia when we got home.

Alicia: On March 17, 1995, my family and I picked up Kulus at the airport. When the airline crate rolled down the belt, I saw a darling little face that I fell in love with immediately. The pup sat in the crate smiling at me, whimpering with excitement and probably a little fear. That's when it hit me. *I'm a mother!* I felt overwhelmed.

Karen: Kulus was seven and a half weeks old when he arrived. Alicia had the idea he would be a live, cuddly, stuffed animal. Kulus was anything but that. He was the dominant male of his litter, and he would try again and again to put Alicia back into the pack. But she stood firm, all three and a half feet of her, and let him know who was boss. She is the youngest puppy trainer in Atlanta, but she's one of the toughest.

The family found that acclimating Kulus was truly a twenty-four-hour-a-day job. Only thirty minutes of formal training daily is required—other than classes and testing—but the dog has to adapt to many different environments, from traffic-jammed streets to the local mall. Alicia took him to school, where he learned to wait quietly under her desk, taking no notice of the other children.

At home he is a family pet. But when he wears his yellow vest, his working uniform, he becomes an animal with a mission, one who loves to work for nothing more than a pat on the head and a "good dog."

He has also become a world-class snuggler. If Alicia or Lucas are home sick from school, Kulus decides he's the best blanket in the house and lays full length on top of them. When Alicia sits on the floor to watch TV, Kully is glued to her side, or draped over her. It's quite a sight, considering the dog weighs ten pounds more than she does.

That dog wormed his way into all our hearts. He even conquered Bob, who had made a valiant effort to keep himself aloof. But it is Alicia whom Kully loves with unrestrained adoration.

I brought him one day to pick her up from school. In about thirty seconds flat, he was surrounded by Alicia's classmates.

"Can I pet him?"

"Can I walk him?"

"Why is he wearing that yellow jacket?"

But Kulus politely and firmly ignored them, never turning his gaze away from the school door. When Alicia emerged, half hidden behind a taller classmate, Kully stood, straining forward, his ears pointed and stiff. I swear he grinned.

When Alicia saw him, she flashed an answering smile, but neither ran to the other. Dog and mistress followed every propriety needed for a well-trained canine helper. Yet the love between them was as visible to me as their smiles.

They are best friends, best companions, working toward a goal that my little girl knows is worth any sacrifice, even though the magnitude of the sacrifice grows with each day.

For the rest of the family, the parting will be just as hard. I look at the two holes in our walls, dented during rambunctious play, or at the occasional damage he and Watson cause roughhousing around the house, and I try to think, *It's good it will be over soon.* But I'm lying to myself. I can hardly fill out his final papers because I'm crying every time I pick up my pen.

Alicia: I know I'll miss him terribly, but there's a part of me bursting with pride. I don't totally understand my feelings, but I suspect it comes from knowing how much help he'll be to someone with a disability.

Karen: If Kully doesn't pass his tests, we have first claim on him. Yet none of us want that. In fact, we're looking forward to his graduation next November. We'll get to see him again, and Alicia will have the honor of presenting him to his future master or mistress.

Alicia: It's so hard to give up something you love. Sometimes I can't even bear to think about it. But I want him to graduate.

Karen: You see, after watching these dogs with their people, we want him to succeed. We know how much it will hurt to put Kully on that plane tomorrow, but none of us, not Bob, Lucas, myself, or Alicia—especially Alicia—has ever given a second thought to the idea of keeping him. He's needed elsewhere.

➤➤➤ • ‹‹‹

Alicia and her family have recently moved to the Northwest. But this won't stop the whole clan from attending Kully's graduation in November. Early reports on the pup indicate fine progress and every hope of success.

Kindred Spirits

The heart has its reasons which reason does not understand.

—Blaise Pascal

The Letters

By Samantha Glen, 47, author

⟨⟨⟨⟨⟨⟨

I'D MADE THIS TRIP SO MANY TIMES I COULD QUOTE THE timetable blindfolded. Leave Kennedy Airport approximately 8 P.M., arrive London, Heathrow, in time for early breakfast. Then catch the train from Waterloo, south to the little tourist town by the sea, and from there it's but a short ride by taxi to the nursing home.

"He's taking a rest on the sun porch," they told me when I arrived. He sat, chin tipped to his chest, folded into himself like a concertina. A shallow snore fluttered vanishing lips. Shafts of pale winter sun stole secretly across his face, exposing the landscape of a hard eighty-five years on this earth.

He seemed shrunken, smaller than I remembered. His eyebrows sprang unkempt and bushy above pouchy lids, giving him the look of some wild cossack. Clumped strands of matching white hair sprouted from his ears. In repose he couldn't disguise the mouth that had collapsed inward, and I wondered if he still bothered with his false teeth. I squatted before him, and stroked a hand networked with corded veins.

"Hello, Dad," I whispered.

There was a long sigh, a startled, barely noticeable shudder before the tired lids flew open and two familiar, yellow-tinged eyes peered into mine.

"Who's that, then?" The question was a demand, with all the remembered belligerence of old. I waited a few seconds before answering so my father could connect me with his memory.

"It's me, Dad. Your daughter, Sam."

"Sam? Sam? I don't know a Sam."

I kept stroking the aged hand, and he flinched but didn't pull away. My brother said that our father still recognized him, although he would insist my brother's young wife was his own Ivy, deceased these fifteen years now.

I was glad my father was here in this place of safety and sunshine. Glad his room was splashed with colors of yellow and blue and had fresh flowers in a vase by his bed. Glad the two sprightly ladies down the hall vied to fetch his morning paper and afternoon toast and tea. Glad to know he ate regularly and had people around him again, although he complained incessantly that they talked too much for his liking.

I give my brother the credit for finding this nursing home so close to the seafront my father liked to stroll on Sunday afternoons. But I give it grudgingly, remembering the pleas and the fights, the sense of helplessness because Richard, a mere one hour and a half's distance from Dad, neglected to take any action for two years. He relied on me, an ocean away, to solve *all* problems.

A painful image of Richard and me, on either side of our father in the middle of a sidewalk thronged with afternoon shoppers, trying to calm the man who flailed with his cane and ranted that we were no children of his. "You deceived me. You said we were going for a nice meal. I don't need a doctor. D'you hear? There's nothing wrong with me. You deceived me. You're no children of mine."

Meanwhile, the calls came from the police station with increasing frequency.

"This is Sergeant Matlock." And my brother knew that my father had been knocking on his neighbor's door at midnight, clad only in shabby pajamas that sorely needed a wash, or had been picked up in the all-night Kentucky Fried Chicken at 3 A.M.

"I'm catching a plane tomorrow. This can't go on," I told my brother after one complaint too many.

Richard couldn't pick me up at the airport—too busy, he said—so I took the train to my hometown and heard the news alone.

"Early dementia," the doctor informed me. "He'll be all right for a while, but I suggest you make some arrangements."

It is a dilemma faced by so many of my generation—a parent whose age betrays them. My brother struggles to support three children and a wife whose sympathy is worn thin by a father-in-law who insults her family.

"Come live with me, Dad," I begged so many times I could chant the chapter and verse of his heated refusal.

In the end we did deceive him, my brother and I. "A holiday while we get the flat repainted," we enthused, as we settled him into a private room in the residence whose staff I had personally vetted. But he'd slip away to try to find his old home. We'd bring him back, and he'd look at me with eyes so filled with reproach I'd turn aside.

I spent many months in the country of my birth that first year. Anger, sorrow, guilt—the emotions buffeted me like a storm in the

English Channel. Anger, at the injustice and humiliation wrought by time on the body and mind, I could understand. Sorrow, to see a man who'd gone through life as obstinate as a goat reduced to such dependence, I could understand. But guilt? For what? I was suddenly another age, another place, twenty-some years gone.

"Why do you want to leave me and your mother?"

"Dad, it's not you. There's nothing for me in this village."

I didn't confess that I wanted some validation—somewhere, from someone—that I was more than the sum of my flesh; that my dignity counted for something; that not every move I made, the way I did my hair, dressed, spoke, was unworthy. I was fleeing from "Who do you think you are?"

→→➤•◄←←

"Wipe your lips, dear." The request was furtive, accompanied by a quick glance around the empty porch, and I returned from my memories. "They're too red, Sam," my father chastised. "Makes your mouth look like a tart's."

The lipstick was pink and I'd eaten most of it off at breakfast. "Yes, Dad." I opened my purse and pulled out a Kleenex to rub off the offending color. At least he recognized me. "I'm taking you to lunch, and then I've got matinee tickets for the ballet."

A frown furrowed two deeper lines between my father's bushy brows. "What's wrong with eating here? It's free."

"You're going out," I said. "I've got reservations at the Merry-wood Manor."

His eyes narrowed, he leaned forward and hooked an index finger in my face. "You got money to burn, girl? If I've told you

once, I've told you a thousand times, you'll never amount to anything, never have a penny to your name, if you carry on like this."

"Yes, Dad."

We had a quiet, companionable afternoon. I watched with
satisfaction as my father ate every morsel of four successive
courses. "Can't have waste." And I smiled at the complaints with
every bite. He fell asleep at the ballet, and didn't know my name
when he woke, but leaned on my arm when we left the theater.
For some reason, that felt good.

Richard was on the phone from London when we got back to
the home. "How is he?"

"I think he's happy. He told me the ladies he likes, and the men
he can't stand. And there's a nurse he's fond of who—"

"Are you going to his flat?" my brother cut in.

"After dinner."

"Don't be shocked, it's a mess. I can't make head or tail of the
paperwork. But you can do it, you're good at that, aren't you?"

"Yes."

→ ⇒ • ⇐ ←

The smell was of old age—musty, dusty, ill used. It hit my nostrils
as the door was unlocked and never left my senses for as long as I
stayed in the two bedroom, one kitchen, one living room with
balcony.

The shock was of drawers stuffed with long ago bills, uncashed
checks, correspondence unanswered, of closets crammed with
boxes of papers and more papers. Of one bedroom floor littered
with envelopes and typewritten pages as if my father had thrown

them down in disgust, or weariness. So many years of neglect, of fighting a disease that sapped a man's intelligence, his energy, his ability to function.

I sighed and put on the kettle for tea. Richard was right. My grasp of business was better than his. Of the two of us, it was I who knew what to keep, what to discard, whom to call and demand an accounting.

"I don't like that raincoat on you, dear," my father said, as we walked the promenade on my third afternoon.

"Yes, Dad. I'll get a new one."

"Makes you look fat, you know."

I saw him to sleep a few hours later, and dragged my exhausted body back to the coldness of a flat that no longer had life. At least, I comforted myself as I faced yet another night of deciphering the threads of my father's world, I was making progress. Another couple of days and I'd have it all sorted out.

It's funny how the most important moments of your life happen at the end of an ordeal . . . or at three o'clock in the morning.

For me it was both. The ordeal was seeing the recalcitrance of a man who would challenge anybody, on anything, just to prove he was right—even if he was wrong—come to an inability to cope with the gas bill.

Three in the morning was when I found the shoe box.

It was actually a box for boots. Its cardboard sides had been reinforced with Scotch tape, and its middle secured twice with slender yellow satin. The ribbon was frayed and faded, but tied in a meticulous bow nonetheless.

The box had been shoved to the back of the wardrobe in the unlived-in bedroom that had been my mother's. Her dresses still hung as if it were yesterday, their pressed folds preserved with the pungency of mothballs. The box had been secreted behind her skirts. I might have almost passed it by, but there it was, another something to be dealt with.

I tore off the ribbon, too tired to really care, and the contents spilled around me on the industrial gray carpet. I wanted to swear because, of course, there was only me to pick them up.

Then I saw my own handwriting on an envelope.

I opened it as if the pages it contained were the curses of Pandora's box, and read a letter written twenty years before. "Oh, Dad, I've met a wonderful man. You'd like him, he plays chess and is very frugal. Just like you."

"Oh, Dad," I wrote a year later, "my love and I are no longer together and . . ." The sad story ran over the pages.

"Oh, Dad," I wrote six months later, "I just got the most fabulous job and am moving to California."

And so it went. The story of my life strewn over a worn carpet in a bedroom vacated after the death of a mother.

I slumped to the floor and curled into myself. My whole being was blank for I don't know how long. One by one, I read each message and counted back through the years. My very first postcard. "Dad, I'm in Majorca. Have you ever been in Majorca?" And, "Dad, I'm in the South of France. Weren't you in France during the war?"

All the journeys of my life, all the loves, hopes, ambitions, triumphs, and disappointments . . . all inked on cards, scribbled on yellow-pad pages or the elegance of embossed notepaper, laser printed as the years went on.

Why, why, had my father kept every letter, note, card, and photograph I had sent through twenty-five years of exile? The question was rhetorical. I knew the answer and wondered why I'd never guessed he loved me so.

A lifetime of past misunderstandings flooded into my consciousness. And I cried for all the lost years between us.

I don't remember the sun telling me it was morning, time to get myself together. I know I gathered up my letters, cards, and photographs and tied them with the frayed, yellow ribbon, knowing I would keep them all my life.

I hugged my father at breakfast and said, "I love you, Dad."

"So what's this all about then?" he said, pulling away. "People are watching."

"I just love you, Dad," I said again. I sat down beside him and ordered kippers and scrambled eggs, for once in my life ignoring the diet that said I should live ten years longer.

"That's better," my father said. "You're too skinny, you know. Men like a bit of something to grab hold of."

"Yes, Dad."

"So when are you coming again?"

"Soon, Dad. Very soon."

Samantha makes it a point to visit her father as often as possible. He now likes to play the piano for the ladies on social nights, albeit, he avers, they still talk too much. Everything has fallen into place for Sam these last few years. She is the happiest she has ever been in her life.

Mrs. Tyler's Story

From Alberta Tyler, 70s, apartment complex manager

꧁꧂

WASHINGTON, D.C., WAS A SLEEPY KIND OF TOWN AFTER the bustle of my native Birmingham, Alabama, with its factories and coal mines. But I was only nineteen, and shy, and this was only my second evening in the city.

I had met a nice girl through my aunt, and she had procured an invitation for me to attend a select party at the home of a woman very prominent in colored society.

My dress was a demure lace and taffeta I used for socials at Bible Memorial College, where I attended school. I adjusted my hat and pulled on my gloves just as my aunt called to me to come.

I remember how lovely the lady's home was. The orchestra played on the terrace, its music filling every room. The food was abundant and delicious. I remember being impressed by my new friend's brother, Ernest, who was our escort for the evening. Especially impressed. Ernest and I later married. But marriage was far from my thoughts on this first evening.

Our hostess introduced me to a room full of girls about my age, then left. Because I was shy, at first I just listened.

There was the usual gossip about other people, some talk of travel plans and school. The girls were nice and tried to include me, and I began to feel comfortable. Then it happened.

"Did you meet Blanche's cousin?" one girl asked, kind of tittering.

"You mean the one from Spartanburg? Lord, yes. We met her."

Everyone began to laugh, and I wondered what was wrong with the poor girl from South Carolina. One young lady turned to me.

"You wouldn't have seen her. She left yesterday."

"You wouldn't have wanted to see her," another chimed in.

"Mush-mouthed, cotton-picking hick. I was surprised she didn't wear her hair in tiny braids all over her head like Prissy in *Gone with the Wind*."

"All those girls from the South are the same."

"Cotton picking and corn shucking."

I glanced from one laughing face to the other. Obviously, these young women had no idea I was from Alabama. Was this truly what they thought of Southerners? I had never seen a cotton field in my life, let alone picked any.

My thoughts turned immediately to my mother. An educated woman, she had attended Morris Brown College in Atlanta, where she majored in music. Churches throughout Alabama clamored for her to come and perform, and not only music. She was a great orator. One year, she was asked to give the commencement speech at Tuskeegee. She sewed the first black dolls anybody had seen in Alabama, and sold them to a company in Chicago.

Cotton picking and corn shucking? Not *my* mother.

"You'd think they believed slavery was still legal," one girl laughed, breaking into my thoughts. "All this 'Yas, ma'am' and 'No, ma'am,' and ducking their heads as if someone was going to whip them."

I couldn't believe their ignorance. Did they truly not realize the tensions black people had to endure in the South? Again my thoughts slipped away to a horrifying story I had heard not too long before.

Mother told of a friend whose son had been lured to the Mississippi Delta by a slick talker in a suit. The people who owned the island were rich, white folks, and they raised cotton and sugar. Once the son hit the island, he was a slave. I mean it. And this only five years before, in the 1930s.

The young man told the other black people who worked there that they were free, that slavery had been over since the Civil War, but they didn't believe him. When the overseers heard what he was saying, they beat him so bad, he almost died.

Now this man could read and write, whereas the other blacks on the island couldn't. One day he escaped by swimming off a deserted stretch of beach and sneaking onto a train full of goats. But they sent men after him and he was caught before he got too far—but not before he got a letter off to his mother.

My mother helped her friend hire two white lawyers, and believe me, they had to get rough to get that son free. I don't know what happened to the other slaves still stuck there. The lawyers only went to court for the man they were paid to fight for, and not until they received their money.

Did any of these silly girls at this lovely party know such nightmares occurred in the South?

"Blanche's cousin was telling me about her brother," one girl giggled, "as if she thought I might be interested."

"I wouldn't date a Southerner if he came wrapped in gold."

By this time I was clenching my teeth so hard I thought I might crack them. My father was a Southerner, and the best man who ever lived. He was a Methodist, and had been asked to step up to be a bishop, but he declined because he wanted to be a presiding elder. He shunned the glory of being a bishop to be able to work among the people instead. He, like my mother, was a man of education, having attended Selma University. My father was truly wrapped in gold—the gold of a generous heart.

"And the way they speak!"

"I don't think English is their language at all."

"Did you hear Blanche's cousin? 'Friend girl' instead of 'girl-friend.'"

"All niggers from the South should be made to stay there, and not bother the rest of us."

Niggers? I couldn't stand it any longer. I don't know what possessed my soul at that moment, but I stood and clapped my hands. "May I have your attention? I want you all to know I'm a native Alabamian."

A terrible hush fell over the room, and they stared at me, their mouths open. They were shifting in their seats, believe me.

"How dare you?" I continued. "How dare you be so ignorant of your own people?"

I felt my proud, educated, refined mother and father right by my side when I sounded off to those girls. I was eloquent with anger, and before I was finished I had shamed them into changing their ideas of Southerners. Before I left the party, all of them apologized.

My parents never minced words, and I learned not to—that night and many times later. They showed me I do not have to bear ignorance and hatred. And I will not.

All through the years, Mother's and Father's example—and my Lord Jesus—have led me down the right course. Because of them, and the strength of mind they endowed to me, I've had a good, full life. For that, I praise my Lord, and thank my parents.

————•————

Mrs. Tyler and her husband, Ernest, still live in Washington. She has managed an apartment complex for more than thirty years, keeping it beautiful and safe. One of her tenants sent her a letter describing her as "a jury, a good lawyer, a doctor, and the best damned manager I've ever had the pleasure to deal with."

Life Support

By *Theresa Mills, 43, magazine publisher*

THE FIRST TIME I MET JULIANA I THOUGHT, *I CAN'T BE friends with someone who has hair like that.* Juliana's hair is a glorious, cover-girl blonde that cascades in thick, heavy, waves halfway down her back. For someone who has struggled with short, wispy hair all her life, that was just too much. But we had an instant rapport, and of course, we did become friends.

I was probably a little intimidated by her the first two years. She would invite my husband and me to a masquerade ball, a mystery party, sledding and sleepovers, movies and trips to New York, as easily as to the local McDonald's. Juliana is a constant whirlwind of ideas, activities, and feelings, especially feelings. She would share with me anything and everything that touched her, made her angry, happy, or sad. I was much more reticent.

Then we started to experience some "real" life together, the birth of our sons, Adam and Michael. Juliana elected to have a natural delivery, and when she was six months pregnant asked if I would be her coach. I was touched and honored and immediately read everything I could find about the coach role in the birth process. Of course, no amount of studying can prepare you for that God-filled, awesome experience. There is something so life-lasting intimate about looking in your friend's face and saying, "Okay, time to push."

It was a long labor to bring her son, Adam, into the world. He weighed in at almost eleven pounds, but the only complaint Juliana uttered was, "Next time, I'll take the epidural." I think both of us were overwhelmed at seeing this miraculous little (well, not so little) boy. That moment of birth united the three of us in a way not to be described.

My own son, Michael, is adopted. Four times I'd gotten pregnant and each time lost the baby. Now I believe that all those years I was trying to have a child, Michael was up in heaven, bouncing around saying, "Wait for me, wait for me."

My husband and I were to pick him up from the hospital when he was two days old. Juliana, of course, hired a white stretch limousine for the trip home.

I remember every moment of that day: walking into the hospital with Juliana's husband following us with a video camera; tip-toeing into the nursery; and finally holding my baby.

"Oh, Theresa, he's so beautiful," Juliana said.

He was and still is. Michael is the single most important thing that ever entered my life, and my friend was there for that grand entrance.

That same year we started a small business together. Looking back, I realize we really didn't know what we were doing, but we're both hard workers and our strengths and weaknesses seem to balance each other. Most important, we've learned that—surprise, surprise—two dedicated women can make sound decisions, can make mistakes, and can still survive in the world of business.

Within months, Juliana was pregnant again. But this was to be a very different birth. In her sixth month, my friend was informed that her baby had died in utero. Once again she called me from the hospital to ask me if I would come to help her through the labor. I couldn't keep back the tears for the perfect little girl who would never open her eyes. I held her in a baby pink blanket, my entire body trembling. The room was gray and quiet, as was Juliana. That moment, too, is etched forever in my memory.

In 1992, within six months of each other, both our husbands filed for divorce. I won't go into the gory details; this story is about us, not them. I will only say that Juliana and I equaled each other in the shock and pain that can only be understood by someone who has lost a person they love, and in that losing discovers that a part of her own self is irrevocably gone.

We are very different people, Juliana and I. She held her head high, made plans, and took action. I went into hiding for a few years. Of course, the end result was the same—we learned to adjust, however painfully, and our lives began to fill up again. But not without a lot of help from family and friends, and for me it was always Juliana by my side when I needed comforting.

We are so close, my friend and I. Oh, we've had some knock-down, drag-out fights, but we never give up on each other. We've had some absolutely hilarious times, some of which are not fit to print. We've had a million conversations about life, God, our beautiful children, and even a few kind words about our former husbands.

Juliana and I walked this morning. It was foggy, and here and there the footpath was covered with treacherous ice that made us clutch each other for support. It's the way it's always been, when I think about it. Juliana and I walking at our slightly different paces, but close enough to grab each other for support when we need it.

I pray that's the way it will always be.

→→➤ • ◄←←

Theresa wrote this story for Juliana's eyes only. She wanted to put in writing how she felt about her friend. By sweet serendipity, the tribute was shown to the authors, who knew it had to be part of this book. And fortunately, Theresa and Juliana agreed.

~~Listen . . .~~

As told to and written by L. M. Azar, 40, *poet*

~~lllllll~~

$\mathcal{M}$Y NAME IS KAY. I AM A TRADITIONAL MEDICINE MAKER and healer, walking the continent in a gesture of hope and a deed of unity. Ahead of me strides Grandfather—Chief William Commanda, leader of all the Algonquin nations. He is straight and tall. His eighty-three years have sculpted a figure humble yet proud. He leads our migration, the Sunbow 5: Walk for the Earth, which began on the shores of Cape Cod and will culminate on the coast of the Pacific.

This historic journey has been organized by Native Americans and others of different races to raise consciousness about the importance of collective unity in the issues of peace between men and environmental well-being.

I am honored to walk behind Grandfather, also known as the Keeper of Sacred Knowledge, a man of prayer and ceremony. He is a man with a vision essential to the well-being of all people, one who speaks in plain terms, not in mysterious or mystical ways. His message rings clear in my thoughts. *We must love one another, pay tribute to our Creator, and take care of our Mother, the Earth. Above all, we must forgive.*

My memories of Grandfather fade into the depths of my childhood in Maniwaki, Quebec. When I was six years old, I fell from an overcrowded van that transported children of the reservation to school. My overcoat snagged the door, and I was dragged for a long time before the vehicle stopped. I couldn't walk. I recall the excruciating pain that blinded my vision, followed by the musky smell and cool sensation of wet leaves being molded to my legs by Grandfather.

I felt his soothing hands, I heard his soft prayers, I felt the strength of his healing. Every day he returned to our home to comfort me with both herbs and prayers.

I feared I might never walk again, but Grandfather assured me that I would walk great distances in my lifetime. He taught me to have faith, and to believe in his healing, which came through our Creator.

With each day that passed, my bones and muscles grew stronger as the flesh of my knees recovered, until once more I could walk and play as before.

As I grew older, Grandfather taught me to confront my fears. He said, "If you are afraid of the snake, you must say hello to the snake and take time to sit and observe, and it won't harm you. This applies to everything in our lives."

Today, as I walk behind Grandfather on this great journey, I hear his words and prophecies, which have guided me toward the truth. Grandfather, the elders, and we who walk with them share the goal of bringing together people of all colors.

At one time we were able to communicate with living things through a spiritual connection. We lived in harmony with the animals and insects and plant life until we started killing them for reasons other than survival. The animals fled and hid from us. We no longer respected them or cared for them as before. They want to talk to us again, and they're coming back now. They want us to stop the killing and pollution so that they may continue to live. They have nowhere else to turn.

In the winter of 1993, Grandfather spoke at the Cry of the Earth Conference at the United Nations in New York. "We are here due to the urgency of the cry of our Mother Earth and the urgency of our concerns for all forms of life. We have agreed to present our Wampum belts, which are a sacred link to the spiritual and physical forces that contain the power and knowledge of life from past to present to future . . . the healing is essential."

As our people walk the continent we are relaying Grandfather's message to all who are open to it, from the Atlantic to the Pacific. In doing so I show my belief in the truth of his words, and I honor him as a man.

We can all hear the cries of the Earth, if we listen.

→→→‑•‑←←←

The Sunbow 5: Walk for the Earth culminated on February 2, 1996, with Grandfather leading a pipe ceremony of closure in Santa Barbara, California.

Asta

From Kevin George, dog trainer and security officer

WHEN I'M ASKED ABOUT MY FAMILY, I ALWAYS INCLUDE ASTA. This is not the name of my mother or father, sister or brother. Asta is not even a person in human terms. Asta is a dog.

I confess I was never of the legions who unashamedly considered their animals family. What need did I have for surrogate "pet kin" when I had perfectly fine human ones? I'm a divorced man with a son—grown now into a robust police officer, six feet tall, and the pride of my heart. Children always steal your heart.

But Asta stole my soul.

It didn't start out that way. Fifteen years ago I was in search of the perfect dog to help patrol the streets of my hometown of Edmonton, Alberta. And I knew exactly what I wanted—the Dutch-trained Belgian Malinois. The Netherlands constabulary is famous for training some of the most powerful, proficient, agile, and aggressive police dogs in the world. Their animal of choice is the Belgian Malinois, a dog who also has the reputation of being faithful to the death.

So I put in my order and waited. Four long years passed before I received word that my dog was on the way. On a September night in 1985, I picked up my cargo at the airport. Forty-five minutes later we were home, and I got my first good look at my prize.

The dog was big. Maybe twenty-seven inches at the shoulder, maybe ninety pounds. He resembled a lion—a great, powerful lion, with a black face and a short coat of reddish brown. "Welcome to your new home, Asta."

Dispassionate brown eyes gleamed at me from the depths of the shipping crate. Asta didn't wag his tail or bark. Asta just stared. Spooky.

"Poor boy, good boy," I soothed, as I opened his crate. I was surprised there wasn't any smell, then I saw why. The inside of his container was spotless. This animal had endured a fourteen-hour flight from Europe to Canada without doing the "doggy thing."

"Go on, Asta," I urged. "I bet you need some relief, boy." But the dog didn't move. Of course, I didn't speak his language. I didn't even know his language. I slapped my hand against my thigh in the universal gesture. "Come." Asta jumped to the ground and padded beside me to the nearest tree. "Go to it, boy."

Asta understood those words all right. He went to it with a vengeance. Every bush and tree in the yard got marked as Asta's territory, yet never once did the dog take his eyes off me. When he'd finally finished I reached out to pat his head, but he showed no response. In my thirty-three years of dog training, I'd never seen anything like it. What was with this animal? He was a far cry from Dox.

Dox was my big Rottweiler—a patrol dog, show champion, and TV star, with a syndicated Canadian series called *Mania*. Dox was my working partner, my grand, old friend, even now waiting in the house to greet me as if I'd been gone for years instead of an hour, and I wanted to join him.

But I knew it wouldn't be fair to take the new dog indoors right away. He had to be stiff as black ice after his journey. I reached out to pat him one more time. Again he jumped out of reach. "I know what you need," I said. "You need some play time." Asta just looked at me like I was nuts. "Try it, what have you got to lose?" I picked up a ball and tossed it.

Asta's ears went up, and his whole body tensed. He tore after the ball, and seconds later was back at my side. "Well, that wasn't so bad, was it?" Then I made a very bad mistake. I tugged at the ball in the dog's mouth, trying to take it away.

I heard the growl deep in his throat but ignored the warning. Asta bit down hard. A second later I felt the full ninety pounds of the dog's weight hurled against my body. My legs buckled and I went down. Just in time, I swung my forearm in front of my face.

Asta's fangs ripped into the leather of my jacket. And as sure as I'd been a policeman for fifteen years, I knew this dog was trying to do me harm big time.

I heard the rip of cloth as Asta tore the heavy denim of my trousers, then he lunged anew for the vulnerability of my face. For the first time in my life I was terrified of a dog. I forced my knees to my chest, thinking I had one faint chance. *Yes! Now!* I thrust forward and the lion dog jackknifed across the grass. "Stay!" I yelled and pointed a finger at Asta's head. The dog dropped, sides heaving as he stared at me through a black mask cold with intent.

I stood up carefully—nothing was broken, thank God. The dog raised his lips, showing pointed fangs. *Faithful to the death? They didn't say whose death. What the hell had I gotten myself into?*

➤➤➤ • ◂◂◂

It took me two years to answer that question. During that time my routine with Asta was unvaried. Evenings, I'd fetch the dog out of his kennel and put him in the security cruiser. Mornings, it was back to the kennel. It wasn't that I was unkind. I liked the dog, treated him with respect. But I kept my distance.

To tell the truth, I didn't need to be close to Asta, I still had Dox. But time was catching up to my grand, old Rotty. In the spring of 1987, my friend, who'd served me without fail, who'd repaid kindness with adoration, passed away in my arms. I cried until my body had no more water left in it.

Asta watched it all.

One night, not long after, as I led Asta back to his kennel following a hard night's patrol, I gave him a perfunctory scratch behind his ears. Asta didn't freeze or back away as usual. Instead he leaned against my fingers, and a warm muzzle nosed cautiously into my palm.

Asta's brown gaze was sad and pleading, not confrontational. In fact, now that I thought of it, he hadn't shown any aggression toward me in some while. For the first time, I didn't see Dox. I gave Asta a rough, two-handed rub, and his tail swiped from side to side.

Suddenly, I understood. Asta had been trained in Holland where police dogs were considered nothing more than well-oiled machines. Praise and affection were alien to most of them. Yet Asta was a living, feeling animal trying to talk to me in the only way he knew, and I'd been blind to it.

"I'm sorry, boy. You want a chance too, don't you?" Asta licked the back of my hand. "I guess that means, 'Yes.'"

With my defenses finally let down, I was open to everything Asta had to offer, although I still thought of the dog in selfish terms. Like the time a tornado ripped through Edmonton, killing thirty people, injuring thousands.

Our city, our province, had never experienced such a disaster. And there was not one team of search and rescue dogs in all of Canada to help us. If people cried for help beneath the rubble, no one could readily hear them. If families pleaded for the remains of their loved ones, no one could readily find them under the collapsed buildings.

Stunned by our helplessness at that moment, I gathered together a group of volunteers and their dogs and we started to form a search group. Asta was born to the work. Because of him, I founded SARDA—the first Search and Rescue Dog Association of Alberta.

It never crossed my mind to ask my dog how he might feel about this. Who ever asked a dog his opinion? I simply knew he would do it, and I was right. Without human hubris, Asta led the way for all of us.

It's been eleven years since the street-hardened police dog became a search and rescue dog. It would take me all day to tell you how many men, women, and children for whom we've searched. How many grieving families to whom my buddy's brought closure.

As for me, Asta has taught lessons in wisdom and emotion I hadn't thought possible from an animal. Asta has worked with me, cried with me, ached with me, protected me, and looked to me for protection. In doing so, he's given me new perspectives. Through his unhesitating courage, he showed me my vulnerabilities. Through his blind loyalty, he's taught me faith. Through his unconditional love, he's allowed me to be tender. Because he accepts me without reservation, with all my faults, he's taught me to be humble and grateful.

My dog is now thirteen years old. His black mask is gray. Arthritis has affected him through the hip and spinal column, and he's finding it hard to move. But Asta's body is the only part of him that is broken. His spirit is still valiant.

In April 1995 the Royal Canadian Mounted Police formulated a nationwide standard for search and rescue dogs. The RCMP's tribute to the dog whose courage and work is famous across Canada was an invitation to be the first to go through the tests.

He worked his little heart out. I had tears in my eyes as I watched, and wanted him to stop. *He* wanted to keep going. He'd run, and fall, and get up and look at me with his tail wagging. "Just a little slip, Dad, don't make me quit now."

Stairs too high? Didn't faze him. Climbs too steep? He attacked them with vigor. Asta located every item in every hiding place. The RCMP presented him with "Certificate Number One," to honor him as the first dog to pass their tests. It was nothing less than old Hokey Pokey deserved.

We're counting the days together now, me and my kid, just being friends, calling each other names. He spends his time at home, chewing his precious cong—a rubber ball that looks like a Dairy Queen ice cream cone—while keeping a lookout for cong burglars. He'll chew that toy until my brains fry, then just look at me and wiggle his tail because he knows that makes more noise. Then Mr. Bad Pup thinks, "Hey, Dad's sitting on this gorgeous couch. Why not lie there with my head on Dad's lap and he can scratch my ears while I chew my cong. It'll drive Dad nuts." He's gone from police dog to search dog to couch dog to his-highness-sprawled-across-my-bed-leaving-Dad-an-inch dog.

Asta can't look after himself anymore. Yet even in these twilight years, he's continued to enlighten me. He's let me see that old ones have young hearts, and it reminds me to be kind.

ASTA

On October 19, 1995, the Canadian government honored us, Asta and me, with the first annual Outstanding Search and Rescue Achievement Award. David Collonette, the minister of defense, presented the plaque to the team in a ceremony that was carried on 125 television stations, including overseas.

I know Asta's getting ready for the path to the final search, and try as I might to prepare myself for that, losing him will be one of the hardest things that's ever happened in my life.

Somewhere, I've read that humans give dogs their spare minutes, their spare food, their spare room. In return, a dog gives them all he has and all he is. That's my kid. My Asta. I've learned as much about the meaning of family from that dog as from any person in my life.

→→→• ←←←

Asta is still enjoying his well-earned retirement. Kevin still leads the Search and Rescue Dog Association of Alberta, a nonprofit organization whose volunteers carry on its work with their own time and efforts. For those interested in more information about this important work, SARDA's address is 7120–91 Street, Edmonton, Alberta, Canada T6E 2Z7.

Remembrances

The past is not
a package one can
lay away.

—Emily Dickinson

Grandma Left Us on a Monday

By Daniel James (D. J.) Cashmere, 9

~~~~~~~

MY GRANDMA, DOTTIE CASHMERE, WAS LIKE A DIAMOND. No matter what way you looked at her, she was almost perfect. Mom tells me she was the President of Brandeis Women's Committee and received the Brandeis Woman of Valor award for everything she did, and helped other people to do.

But what I remember best is she always stuck up for me. It was like she knew when I was having a bad day at school, or was about to get into trouble. I'd see her car waiting in the parking lot, and knew we'd get an ice cream cone and talk.

She was born on January 24, 1939, and died on May 8, 1995.

Grandma was so brave. She fought the cancer very hard, and kept getting up again. Even though she was on chemotherapy for a long time, she still went white-water rafting. She'd have sleepovers for me, my brother, and my cousins, as well as parties with my friends. My brother and I found out after she died that she used to sneak out early in the mornings for her treatments so that she could return before we awoke. She did not want to upset us.

One day she couldn't get up anymore. We'd sit on her bed in the hospital to play and talk. She always had presents waiting for us, hidden in the drawers of the nightstand. In April she let us have an Easter egg hunt in her room. That was fun. She sure enjoyed it when we laughed.

I didn't know I had such a short time to be with her. I thought we'd always be together. But she kept getting sicker.

Grandma left us on a Monday.

This is a little poem I wrote that was read at her funeral:

Grandma's Death
by D. J. Cashmere

I wish her not to be dead,
But if she must,
Let her rest her head,
And be happy,
In Thy heavens.

→→→• ←←←

Daniel James Cashmere is a student at Forest Edge Elementary. He loves to play soccer and read. Mysteries and westerns are his favorites. Daniel is considered a big brother by all the kids in his neighborhood.

The Legacy

From Andrea Levy, 39, president, human resources company

IN THE LATE 1970S, I WAS A SALES REP FOR A COMPUTER service company in Philadelphia. It was a good job as jobs go, although the hustling around town to meet with clients all day long could get you down sometimes.

But there was one journey I loved to take. Three, maybe four times a week, as the rush hour traffic thinned out at the end of the business day, I'd nose my white Honda Civic onto I-95 for the drive to Shalom House. I was going to visit Mom-Mom.

Mom-Mom was my grandmother Tillie. She was this gritty, little fighter person, at her tallest maybe five feet with a 40D chest. She used to call herself a meat packer because she worked in the bra and girdle section of Litt Bros. Department Store.

More often than not on these trips, I'd have a companion in the passenger seat: Mischa, my eighty-five-pound Samoyed. Mom-Mom loved dogs and she was especially fond of my imposing white bear of a dog.

I don't know why Mom-Mom loved animals so. I don't remember her ever having any of her own. There was never enough money to go 'round for the family, let alone a dog or cat.

Mom-Mom had never known anything but being poor. She was born in 1897 of Russian Jewish immigrants, and grew up not far from the famous Elfreth's Alley, where Betsy Ross sewed the flag. By the age of thirteen, she was working as a seamstress in a sweat shop.

She married young, as they did in those days, and she and Pop ran a tiny, corner "everything" store they kept open from seven in the morning until ten at night. Pop died too soon and that's when Tillie went to work at Litt Bros. She worked in the bra and girdle department for the next twenty-five years. It was only much later that I discovered she'd forged the age on her birth certificate so they couldn't retire her.

I was thinking about this as my car zoomed past the row houses, older factories, and industrial areas that lined the freeways of northeast Philly. I couldn't imagine working anywhere for two decades.

Shalom House was a nondescript white building on the outside, but you walked into a big, bright room scattered with aging, soft-cushioned chairs and sofas that squashed down when you sat in them. Never once did I enter that lobby without seeing a shining smile light up Mom-Mom's face. Tonight was no exception.

"Andy, you brought Mischa. Come here, boy, I'm over here."

Mom-Mom was in her usual place—a grand, winged chair where she liked to hold court.

She was in an impeccable two-piece outfit of her favorite pale pink. Silver-gray hair waved back from a face remarkably free of wrinkles. It showed off to perfection the faux pearl necklace and matching studs that dotted her lobes. The other retirees might shuffle around in their dressing gowns—but not Mom-Mom.

"Here, Andy, here." She patted the giant paisley ottoman beside her. "Sit down. I've saved your place. You come here, Mischa, boy." She and my dog properly greeted one another with great, wet smooches. "Now you should tell me all about your day, Andy. Nothing left out," she said, wiping her face with a white lace handkerchief.

I wiggled my body into a comfortable position, and got ready for today's story. "I went to see a new client this morning. He had an interesting concept." And I explained to Mom-Mom the man's far-fetched belief that there would be a computer in every home before the end of the century.

As I talked people came and went around us. The director of the home stopped to remind Mom-Mom that she'd promised to sing at their concert tomorrow night. "*Fiddler on the Roof*, Tillie. You've got to sing *Fiddler on the Roof* for us."

Mom-Mom's face creased into a delighted grin. *Fiddler* was her favorite musical. She knew every note of every song. I got a sudden flash of her at a last Bar Mitzvah before she came to Shalom House. She stood in front of the band, her stout little body laced tight in an old-fashioned corset, waving her arms and exhorting all the guests to sing along. Everyone joined in. There wasn't a face without a smile in that room.

"Stay. Hear what my Andy just found out. You'll never believe," she said when they'd agreed on the songs. Her bright smile turned on me, and I obligingly began my story again.

Ned, the janitor, was the next to come by. "I fixed the faucet in your sink, Tillie," he said. "Should work fine now. You let me know anything else you need."

Mom-Mom grabbed his hand and bestowed a look of genuine gratitude on the man. Then she asked, "Ned, how's your wife? Any better?" And Ned told us all about his Joan and her arthritis.

"Tillie, it's time, the sunset," a cheerful voice called. A woman of my grandmother's generation was standing by the door.

"We're coming, Rose," Mom-Mom answered, pushing herself up.

It seemed right that all of us, including Mischa, follow Mom-Mom outside.

The heavens put on a show for us this night, smearing the sky with alternating bands of crimson, rose, and yellow. "Isn't that the most beautiful sunset you ever saw?" Mom-Mom sighed to no one in particular. By now our little group had swollen to seven people.

"Ah yes, the most glorious," another friend of Mom-Mom's, Esther, agreed.

"What are you smiling about, Andy?" Mom-Mom asked.

"I was thinking about the vacation I took in Cancun last year. The sunsets were truly awesome."

"Ah, the pop on the sea," she said.

I'd shared with Mom-Mom how one night a friend had taken me out on his boat and told me to watch the horizon. As the sun dropped below the edge of the world, the ocean was lit by a luminous blue-green flash.

It was amazing, something I'd never seen before. I'd had to call my parents as soon as I got in. Before I even began to tell them, they were laughing and my father said, "Yes, Andy, we know, you just saw the most magnificent sunset." And I remembered I'd always called my parents if it was a particularly beautiful sunset, and I'd always used Mom-Mom's words.

"I appreciate sunsets because of you," I told her.

We stayed outside Shalom House until the last glow of color had faded into inky blue, then it was time for supper. Mom-Mom insisted I stay because they were serving Kamish bread, a very special treat, to celebrate Esther's birthday. "I gave them my recipe," Mom-Mom confided as we trooped back inside. A sweet taste of Mom-Mom's creation came into my memory.

The family used to have Jewish holidays at her house, and she'd make the greatest bread, enough for an army, so there'd be plenty left for us to take home. I'd see her break off a piece at the end of a meal, close her eyes, and savor it like it was the most expensive caviar. I'd eaten bread, all kinds of bread, like that for years after watching my grandmother . . . and it did make it taste better.

The director and Ned took their leave, but the round table for twelve filled up right away. Every other table in the spacious room had a spare seat or two—but not ours. Everyone, it seemed, wanted to dine with Mom-Mom. And I smiled to see more than one person close their eyes as they took that first bite of bread.

I was in a reflective mood tonight. A woman who reminded me of my mother stopped by Mom-Mom's chair. "We missed you yesterday at the outing. Where were you?" The woman was not asking out of politeness. She curled over Mom-Mom, her hand leaning on the armrest, every bend of her body language saying Tillie was someone she cared about.

And I remembered how much my own mother loved Mom-Mom. Daughter, my grandmother always called her. Daughter-in-law was not part of her vocabulary—Mom-Mom never used words that would designate anyone as less of a member of her family.

It came to me then that I was wrong about some things. Mom-Mom wasn't poor. She was the richest person I'd ever known. She gave love in abundance, whether he or she be janitor or president. She shared the small joys in life with everyone around her. To Mom-Mom every day was a gift.

I tried to remember. Had I ever seen her down? Yeah. And hurt? Sure. But she'd always insisted you couldn't dwell on it. "You gotta believe the best in people, Andy." To Mom-Mom that was the only way to live.

I made up my mind in that moment, around that supper table, that I wanted to be remembered like her. In my work—no matter what it might be—and the way I lived my life, I wanted to touch people, or have an impact like Mom-Mom. She was a person whose legacy I wanted to try to live out.

I drove home happier than I'd been in a long time that night. Mischa and I would see Mom-Mom again before the week was out. And hopefully I'd be making this journey for many more years. I needed time to learn the legacy.

→→→•←←←

Mom-Mom died on a gorgeous January Sunday in 1986. One of those days when everything is really sparkly. It was fitting. Mom-Mom had sparkled all her life.

Like Mother, Like Daughter

From Olivia Walsh, 50, administrative assistant

𝓜Y MOTHER'S NAME WAS JOSEPHINE. EVERYBODY CALLED her Josie for short. My earliest memories are of being warm and held. Even when I was a teenager, Josie never irritated me, we never battled, I never thought she was "not cool," in the vernacular of my generation. I only remember loving her—she was a goddess in my eyes—this mother who loved me so much.

She arrived in this country from Italy when she was six years old. As all young Italian girls in her neighborhood did in those days, she sat at her mother's knee and learned the needle arts. By the time she was a young woman, she was an accomplished tailor of men's suits. I like to think my talent and joy in sewing party dresses and costumes for my nieces and nephews comes from Josie.

She was all that was beautiful in the Italian tradition. Small, not more than five foot two, weighing about 100 pounds, with rich olive skin and dark brown hair. I like to fantasize it was her bangle earrings and exotic turbans that first attracted my father. He was an ardent, persistent suitor, dazzled by her presence.

She married my dad when she was twenty, and I came along shortly afterward. She said I almost got stuck with the name Olive because she ate so many when she was pregnant, but no daughter of hers would be named after a fruit, no matter how delicious. So I was christened Olivia.

If happiness is through food, then Josie's family was the happiest in all of South Philadelphia. Sundays at our house were filled with friends and family who would start arriving at noon. All day long she would bring out great bowls of *ossi bucchi gremolata,* a mixture of anchovies, lemon rind, and parsley sprinkled over veal shanks. Green salads and garlic bread accompanied the ongoing thanks for our day of rest, to be followed by her mouth-watering cannoli stuffed with ricotta and pistachio nuts or her sweet *miascia* bread and fruit pudding.

I remember my grandfather would bring his home-brewed red wine and she would mix it with 7-Up for me—to introduce me to one of the joys of living, she said. My mother was a true free spirit, the life of every party with her sharp sense of humor and love of good times. I have watched many a carpet rolled up and music started for the dancing that would invariably be part of the evening. I like to think that continuing the tradition of classic Italian meals for my family and in baking *biscotti Di Prato,* the almond biscuits that my friends so adore, I take after my mother.

I moved to Washington, D.C., from our Philadelphia home when I got married, but it didn't lessen the intimacy between my mother and me. We'd spend every holiday together and would talk on the phone every single night.

I am told it was not good we were so close, although you would have to fight me on that assumption, because one cold,

cold, wintery February day, her voice was not happy. "Livy," she said, "I have such a big lump in my breast. The doctor said it's not good."

I dragged myself to work the next morning, but had to run to the bathroom every half an hour to compose myself. I couldn't concentrate and made so many mistakes, my boss of fifteen years insisted that he put me on the next plane to Philadelphia.

"Go be with her, Olivia. We'll be okay 'til you get back."

I sat outside the hospital room while they performed the eight-hour surgery and prayed she wouldn't die. I was so scared I was going to lose her.

When I saw her deformed body after the surgery, I cried again, but Josie just held my hand tightly and hugged me close. "Well, at least this time the size of my bust will be my choice."

I tried to smile, remembering how my mother had always said it was such a relief to take off her brassiere at the end of the day.

"Livy, be thankful you've got small ones. Look at what these straps do to a woman." And she'd ease the elastic bands off her shoulders to reveal the sore, pink imprints in the flesh.

She got out of the hospital two days early. "I just want to get on with my life," she said.

The first thing Josie did when she felt up to it was hold a "here's to life" party. More than fifty people crowded into her house that weekend. Josie and I cooked for them all, as usual. Only I and my dad knew she had a drainage bag under her housecoat.

Then she confided that she'd joined a volunteer group to help other women cope with the reality of their cancer. "Can't spend all day feeling sorry for yourself," she'd say. "There's a lot of women out there who could do with some cheering up."

Josie fought her cancer with all the spirit with which she lived her life. But the disease was too advanced and she died on Thanksgiving Day that same year. Her death was indescribable to me. What did God have in mind to take this wonderful woman away from all who loved and needed her? I had difficulty dealing with the anger and bitterness.

It took therapy to help me come to terms with my grief and to realize it was a natural process. I like to think that I pulled myself together because Josie had taught me that to grieve too long was harmful, that when she was gone I had to carry on with my life for both myself and those around me. "You can't be sad, Livy," she said. "Life's too short."

It was uncanny. Almost five years to the day, I felt a lump in my own breast. I panicked but thought, as my mother had, that I would be fine. Her last words as she lay dying were that she'd prayed to Our Lord that I wouldn't get the disease. "I never will," I vowed, holding her frail hand as she slipped away.

The diagnosis was, of course, the same. I had breast cancer, just like Josie. Immediate mastectomy was recommend—just as in my mother's case. Within a week I underwent the same surgery as she.

Because she'd died so quickly, I was terrified. Then I remembered how brave she had been, how she had lived life to the fullest until the end. And it gave me strength.

My mother had a saying I'd like to share. "We only have today, Livy. When we close our eyes on the pillow, you can just throw the day in the trash can. It will never come this way again. So live and find joy. All we have are the moments of our lives."

I have never forgotten her words and am truly living every day. Like Josie, I am surrounded with tremendous love, support, and understanding from those who care for me.

I will overcome.

→→➤• ◄◄←

Because of early detection, the doctors tell Olivia she has a 95 percent chance for survival. Like her mother before her, Olivia has joined a group to support other women and share with them Josie's fighting attitude for life.

If Only I'd Told You
I Loved You

From *Peter Carley, 56, engineer and bread baker, as told to and written by* L.M. *Azar, 40, poet*

I WAS BORN AT THE SALVATION ARMY HOSPITAL IN LONDON in 1940, during an air raid. Mary, my mother, delivered me at the time of a bombing, and the nurses suggested she call me Peter, a most popular name at that time. So I became known as Peter the Great, a big name for such a tiny baby.

We lived on the bottom floor of a small row house in the heart of London, Mum and I. Father was a flyer with the Royal Air Force, and stayed at his base in remote Norfolk. Mum was the only person in my life, the only glow in that narrow, dark, cold flat. She was my playmate, a hand to hold when we went to see the ducks in the park, my protector and comforter when the sirens blared their warnings of enemy bombers.

We didn't go out at night due to the blackout. Cheerless evenings were best spent in bed. I'd hug Mum's back as we lay in the dark trying to keep warm. She called me her "little heater."

Often we were awakened in the middle of the night by the drone of overhead planes, and the whistle of falling bombs as they detonated around London. Sometimes we would go outside and watch

256

the searchlights capture the enemy in their white, sweeping beam, then the ground gunners would open up. Once an undetonated bomb fell in our backyard, blowing in the bedroom windows and slicing right through the garden shed. It left one side a pile of clay and the other half untouched, paint cans and garden tools all neatly arranged.

Every war wife dreaded the coming of the blue-uniformed, motorcycle messenger, for his was the dismal job of notifying the next of kin about their loved ones missing in action, presumed dead. I remember Mum sitting at the kitchen table, the yellow telegraph paper stretched across her hands, shaking her head in denial, shoulders heaving. Her beloved husband, my father, robbed from us at the age of twenty-six.

I was the only son of a dead war hero. My grandparents grieved hard and unceasingly, their hearts broken. They lived with memories and photographs and tears. Their child's good looks, personality, ambitions, and life were gone forever.

With the loss of their son, my grandparents moved all their attention to me. "Oh, he's just like Harry," they would say and praise everything I did. They spoiled me as they indulged me with their love.

So I became my mother's companion, her helper, and protector of the family. There were the three of us now, with my little sister, Anne, whom my father never saw. I was now the man of the house, at the age of five. Feeling the responsibility of my new position, I would say, "Here, I'll do that, Mum. It's man's work."

As I grew, the image of my father expanded in my mind. He became a flying ace, a daredevil, a man who died serving his country, a proudly worn uniform with "wings." I was honored to be his son and wanted to be just like him, my father, whom I knew only secondhand.

The years passed, and eventually Mum met another man, Ernest. I don't know when or where Mother met him, but when we left our tiny flat in London to move to the suburbs, Ernest came with us. He was "Uncle" to Anne and me, a man I didn't know and whose presence I couldn't understand.

I resented Uncle. He appeared out of the blue, took my mother's attention, and I felt as if I'd been shoved aside. I saw him unfit to take my father's place. He was not a war hero. I couldn't respect him because he had never gone to war. It wasn't 'til much later that I learned of Uncle's poor health, which exempted him from service.

I refused to listen, obey, or acknowledge Ernest in any way. "Little Harry" didn't want Uncle around. Mum was forced to take the middle of the road to keep harmony in our household. My childhood and teenage years were filled with anger, unhappiness, and confusion.

Uncle tried everything he knew to unite us. He took the family on vacations to the sea, to the rocky coast of Devon and Cornwall. We fished by the shore and ate fresh cream from a nearby farm. At night we lay in bed and watched the Eddystone Lighthouse blinking out to the black depths. But I could never find it within me to forgive Uncle for taking the place of my father, and refused to yield to his affections.

I left home at eighteen, moving far away from England. My growing-up pains became buried in the excitement of my new life, new friends, and new experiences. It wasn't long before I married and started my own family.

The letters from home were frequent and always in Uncle's meticulous handwriting. He would describe the dog becoming old and gray, my sister's graduation from high school, how he and

Mum had landscaped the garden, and he had built little rock walls and a patio with blue albresia hanging and fragrant roses of all colors along the fences. He talked about how they sat outside in the summer evenings and chatted and smoked and drank Cinzano. His letters were clever and poetic, with undertones of his unhidden devotion to Mum. They were companions, best friends, a couple.

It wasn't until I had my own family and felt buried under the responsibility of providing for a wife and five children that I realized how generous and kind a man Uncle had been to me, my sister, and Mum. He never showed any resentment for the difficulty I caused him. That was not his nature. From him came only wishes of well-being and good fortune for myself and my family.

I found myself repeating lessons with my own children that Uncle had once taught me. I reflected on his goodness quite often as a parent, but was never able to verbally express my affection.

The last time I saw Ernest he was lying in bed, thin and pale, with that exaggerated, hollow smile that people show when they are trying so hard to look well. I walked away from Ernest in that state, never sharing that I had grown to love and respect him. Instead I left in silence.

Shortly after I returned to the States, I received a letter from Mum that started, "This is the hardest letter I have ever had to write . . . ."

I have a lasting memory of Ernest, sitting at the piano, cigarette dangling from his lips, looking adoringly at my mother and singing "The Rose of Tralee": "She was lovely and fair, like the roses of the summer. / It was not her beauty alone that won me. / Oh was the truth in her eyes ever yearning, / that made me love Mary, my rose of Tralee."

Unfortunately, I can't turn back the clock. I long to share with Ernest how important he was to my life and how I really loved him for so many years, but was too stubborn to let him know. I see now that this fine man was a fighter to the end. He lived right, he lived morally, he lived without malice.

→→➤•◀←←

Ernest died in November 1965. Mary died twenty-seven years later, in January 1992. She shared her life with no other man after her beloved Ernest's death.

Traditions

*Custom, then, is
the great guide
to human life.*

—David Hume

The Flag in the Canyon

From Mike Paddock, 47, mechanic, and Steve Kibler, 47, computer engineer

᚛᚜᚛᚜᚛

$\mathscr{I}$T WAS AN INCREDIBLE SUMMER, THAT YEAR OF 1967. ONE OF those magical times you get once in a great while, especially if you're a couple of brash, carefree teenagers bent on having a good time.

That's how it was with Mike and Steve before Vietnam. The two eighteen-year-olds had just graduated high school and were rooming together in Glenwood Springs, Colorado, the town where Doc Holliday died. Mike worked in the local lumberyard, and Steve pumped gas, but that's not what it was all about for a couple of best friends on the brink of manhood. For them, real life was hiking up and rapelling down the face of every mountain within ten miles of Grand Avenue and their apartment on top of a bicycle shop.

They chose their venue well. Glenwood Springs lies at the Western terminus of a canyon that straddles Interstate 70 between Vail and Grand Junction. It is a place of terrible beauty where gray granite cliffs spike into clean skies before dropping their slivered sides into the whitewater river that spans its length. Slicing deep into the brooding backcountry are creeks named Grizzly, Devil's

Hole, Defiance, and Deadman, testaments to the turbulent history forged by earlier adventurers to the West.

Mike and Steve made the canyon their own that summer of 1967. There was a certain rock promontory they both liked. It jutted out, separated from the main cliffs by a thin ridge of rock. On clear days a small square of sky wrapped around it like a blue frame around a picture.

In the new year, the army sent Mike his draft notice. Steve, who preferred the technical to the physical, enlisted in the Air Force before the military could send him his induction papers.

Neither of the boys were particularly worried. They had grown up in the one-street town of Palisade. Everybody knew everyone else in this sheltered, little paradise. It was a place where nothing could hurt you. "Back then," Steve reflected later, "we weren't astute enough to know what was really going on across an ocean thousands of miles away."

Yet there was a sense of something, sadness perhaps, that these magic years were coming to a close. One late February afternoon the two friends, whose blonde, good looks could make people mistake them for brothers, slouched over black coffee in their favorite downtown restaurant. It got dark early this time of year, and their mood matched the season. Outside the sky was that deep, mewling leaden that comes before a bad snow, when all the locals run to the store because they know they'll be trapped inside for two days.

"Three weeks before we're outta here," Steve said.

Mike stared into his mug and the silence lengthened.

"Should be quite an adventure," Steve continued.

"Not half as good as what we got here."

"Yeah."

Mike drained his mug and wiped his mouth. "It's just the weather. We need to do something crazy, that's all."

"Why don't we?"

"Yeah. Right. Like the bridge?" The last time Mike had said yes to one of his buddy's ideas, they'd ended up rapelling off the bridge at the edge of town and getting caught by the sheriff. Fortunately, the officer of the law didn't see much harm in the escapade and the boys had gotten away with a stern lecture.

"Wouldn't it be neat to leave a little something for people to remember us by?" Steve persisted.

Mike didn't answer right away. He liked to think things through. "It's got to be something to do with climbing."

Steve nodded. "Yeah. And something to do with our rock."

Mike didn't hesitate this time. "We'll raise the flag," he said quietly.

"Perfect."

→→➤•◄←←

The pole was easy. Mike got that from the lumber yard. The flag presented a different problem. It had to be big enough for them to be able to glimpse it from the road when they climbed down, and strong enough to stand up to the gales that tore through the canyon with depressing regularity.

They scoured every gift shop and hardware store from Vail to Aspen. The only flags they could find were woven from thin cotton, the kind meant for a Fourth of July celebration—not the ferocious winds that ripped the sides of a mountain like it was so much cotton candy.

They used to hang out at a restaurant in town, and knew the owner's daughter. "You guys," the young woman said, "just get two flags and I'll stitch them together. That way you got a shot they might last the winter."

And so it was done. Now all Steve and Mike had to do was wait for a break in the weather.

March 1968 was one of the worst in history: blizzards and record snowfall accompanied by bitter cold. The Ides seemed as good a day as any that year. Mike and Steve crossed the frozen river and worked their way through drifts high as their bellies, and up their ice-covered rock, dragging the flagpole and packs filled with tools.

The snow blinded them and the wind tore at their parkas as they climbed, but they made it to the top, drilled the hole for the pole and guidewires, and hoisted their flag. Fat, wet flakes swirled around the silence, and a sense of wonder came over them. They'd done it. No matter what happened next, they had left their mark.

Steve was the first to come back on leave. By February 1969 he was a year older, and somewhat wiser. Now he knew that his best friend was fighting in a place that wasn't very damn safe. Steve didn't admit to himself that what had begun on a whim already had a deeper significance for him. The symbol of that friendship stood shredded on a pinnacle of rock. He bought another flag— larger, and made of strong canvas this time—climbed their rock, took down the tatters the wind had deigned to leave, and raised a new Old Glory in their place.

Next year it was Mike's turn to come home. He hiked along the canyon floor until he could see the rock spire. The new flag's ragged remains flapped forlornly in its frame of sky. It made him feel kind of sad, like a piece of his boyhood had frayed. He persuaded a couple of local buddies to join him, and together they climbed the promontory and raised a new symbol of their country.

In a miracle for their times, both men survived Vietnam. Soon both were married. Mike settled in Rifle, about thirty miles from their spire. Steve found his home in a suburb of Denver. But by now the flag had taken on a life of its own. What had started as a teenager's silly lark, a one-time act, had become the first real sense of their connection as best friends. What they needed to do from then on was never discussed. One would get on the telephone to the other. "The flag's calling." And they knew it was time to make the climb again.

It has become a yearly pilgrimage. At first it was just wives, children, and close friends who joined the men. Now every year more friends, both old and new, ask to come along. They tell Mike and Steve that making the climb and replacing the Stars and Stripes somehow touches them deep inside, makes them feel closer to their own families and friends.

Somewhere along the way a tradition got started. Each new person who makes the climb gets to keep the old flag. Some have treasured them for fifteen, twenty years, proud to have helped forge what they perceive is a bit of local American folklore.

For the two who started it, the meaning of their climb has changed over the years. For Mike the flag has become a statement. "I love my country and I'm proud to be an American. Steve and I may not have known it at the time, but we put up the flag because it represents everything good about our land."

For Steve it's also about friendship. "Friends have come and gone over the years, but Mike is a constant. We don't talk a lot nowadays, but we have an incredible friendship based on respect—for each other, and each other's expertise. Mike was part of my magic years from sixteen to nineteen."

Mike and Steve are in their late forties now. The tradition hasn't gotten any easier. As Steve says, "I stand at the bottom of the rock after we've made the climb, look up, and see the wind rippling our flag in its frame of dark blue sky. My legs are tired and my feet hurt. But there it is . . . another year. You can't help feeling satisfied. Mike and I will keep putting up a new flag for as long as we're able."

And as long as they do, people will see and exclaim and wonder about the flag that flies alone over this wild stretch of canyon.

———➤ • ◅———

One day after Mike and Steve made their climb in July 1994, the most devastating fires in the area's history broke out. Seven firefighters died containing the Glenwood blaze. That year the men dedicated the flag to their memory. It's their one and only dedication.

The authors wish to thank Mr. Gary Dickson and the staff of the Glenwood Post for their help in locating Mike and Steve and providing background information.

Blackberry Mornings

As told to Mary and Samantha

⁂

A SUMMER SUNRISE WAS BLOOMING IN THE EAST WHEN Mom roused my brothers and me from our beds. "Rise and shine. Up and at 'em. We're going on a treasure hunt."

That woke us up!

"Wow! Chests loaded with pieces of eight from a pirate's map," Mike said, having no idea what pieces of eight might be.

"Pirates? Yeah, right," John interjected, with the scorn of the firstborn.

Baby Jim rubbed the sleep from his eyes. "Toys?"

I stood in their doorway, my nightie tickling my ankles. "Candy," I breathed, not too loudly because I knew I'd be teased.

"Nope. Wild blackberries," Mom stated.

———•———

Outside, the dawn steeped the world in smells of mint and clover, and the grass was silver-green under its dewy cover. Our footprints dotted the lawn like criss-crossing chains of emeralds as we began our quest. Within minutes, we came to bramble-covered hills and discovered our bounty.

At first, in the cool of the morning, it was fun. But as the sun rose, the heat turned the hill into a Sahara, and the brambles whipped our arms with nasty scrapes. "Don't we have enough, Mom?" was followed by, "I'm hot." "I'm thirsty."

Finally, when our bowls were brimming and our fingers and lips stained blue, Mom gave the signal to head home.

The rest of the day was spent in a hot kitchen with an unbending taskmaster. We washed the berries, stirred the jam pot, rolled the pie crusts, none of us allowed to leave until the last jar was filled with midnight nectar.

Who could imagine treasure hunting was such hard work? Finally, our jobs were finished. And the reward was from heaven itself—fresh bread, dripping with blackberry jam, and golden, bubbly pies warm from the white enamel oven.

Mom waited until we were sated from the feast. "Do you know why we do this every year?" she'd ask. We were too tired and too stuffed to answer. "I want you to know," she'd continue, "that the fruits of your hardest labors are always the sweetest." And even through the fog of our sticky, sated content, we understood.

→→→ • ←←←

The storyteller wanted this lesson to be learned by her own children. So, on certain summer mornings, her kids awaken early from their beds to find those disappearing patches of berries. The girls protest—just like the storyteller did—until it's time to eat. Then they understand—just like she did. Those summer evenings, she realizes anew that her mom was a wise woman.

The Gathering

As told to Samantha and Mary

ℰℰℰℰℰℰℰ

CHRISTMAS WAS THE ZENITH OF MY KID YEAR. ALL ELSE orbited in pale comparison—even birthdays couldn't top the magic combination of aromas, sights, sounds, and anticipation. Our house would smell of evergreen, turkey, and pumpkin pies. Church would be crowded with worshipers and filled with red poinsettias. Being the only girl, and an obliging middle child, I'd set the table for Mom using the good china, the Grand Baroque sterling silver, and the French lace cloth.

On Christmas morning my brothers and I would run downstairs after a near-sleepless night to find four neat piles of presents, equal in height and number. My parents would smile at our oohs and aahs and all would agree that Santa was a wonder.

And there was no doubt that Christmas would always be the same. Jeff, Brian, Joey, and I would always be the same. Our parents would always be the same.

"Always" lasted until we grew, married, and scattered to the far corners of the country in a modern diaspora of business reality. We remained close, but what with parents-in-law, siblings-in-law, nieces, and nephews, who had time for all of us to gather as a family?

In September my dad almost died. It was a wake-up call of the worst kind. As he slowly recovered, I realized the family had to come together now, or we might never have the chance again. As I calculated back, it had been more than a decade since all of us had celebrated Christmas under one roof.

That fall morning I was on the phone. In five minutes all three of my brothers and their wives agreed—what a lovely inspired idea—we would spend this holiday at Mom and Dad's house and it would be a gathering to remember. We'd get there a few days early and our parents would have to do nothing. We'd decorate. We'd cook. We'd clean up. Mom and Dad could sit back and enjoy their grandchildren.

Then the reality of living in 1990s nanoseconds struck.

"You guys should come to Los Angeles," my brother Brian proposed in his best physician's voice.

"Are you and Janice backing out?"

"No, I just think everyone should come here. It's warm. It's . . . " He groped hard for something else that might make L.A. appealing at Christmas. "It's . . . warm."

"Mom and Dad can't travel yet," I reminded him.

"But I'll have to buy winter clothes for the kids. They'll only wear them for a week."

"Are you getting cheap on me? You're a doctor for goodness sake. A plastic surgeon in Beverly Hills! Don't tell me you can't afford some new clothes for your kids."

"It's not the money. We have no time!"

"Oh, and I do?"

Brian had the good sense to remain silent.

"Well?"

"All right, all right, we'll come to Boston."

Mom rang me the next day. "Brian and Janice want to take the kids to *The Nutcracker*. You want to go?"

"Of course. But Mom, we can't be there until late Friday night, and that only gives us Saturday and Sunday to do all the decorating, wrapping, last-minute shopping, and cooking. We won't have time to go to the ballet until after Christmas."

"No problem." She paused. "Your dad and I are so happy everyone's coming. I can see Dad getting better simply with anticipation. We can't wait."

Her words made me smile inside. "Neither can we, Mom."

The glow lasted until Jeff, my oldest brother, hooked up with me not twenty-four hours later. His deep, even voice rumbled across the miles in his best no-nonsense attorney style.

"Why did you tell Mom we're not interested in *The Nutcracker?* Betts and I want to take our kids, too."

"Where did you get that from?"

"Mom said we wouldn't have time because we had to do the grocery shopping. I don't appreciate being delegated the gofer in the family, you know."

"You're coming two days before the rest of us. You're the only ones with *time* to do it. Besides, Betts volunteered, and we're splitting the costs."

"I don't care about the money. I wanted to go to the Cape and this messes me up."

My phone hit the cradle with tremendous force. Where, oh where, was my dream of an idyllic family Christmas? After a few deep breaths, I calmed down. This pettiness would pass, I reassured myself. Just the craziness of the season, right?

My next duty was to call around Boston for Christmas dinner reservations, taking into account the requirements leveled at me by various members of the family.

Brian: "I'm the one with four kids, the last thing I need is a long drive. Oh, and no buffets."

Jeff: "We want good food in a pretty setting, I don't care about the expense. And absolutely no buffets."

Joey: "We gotta have turkey leftovers. How about a buffet?"

I wasted many precious hours in consultation with various and sundry before booking the family at a lovely hotel, approved by all—so I thought.

Many days and many phone calls later, a battle-royal had taken shape over the *dinner reservations!* I was seething. "We're staying home," I ranted. "This is ridiculous."

"Mom, we have to go," one daughter begged.

"I've been looking forward to this all my life," her sister wailed.

An exaggeration to be sure, but I knew my girls had been counting the days. They loved any opportunity to be with their cousins. "All right, all right," I said. "But I won't enjoy it!"

Everything seemed against us. The day before we were to leave, the flu struck down my husband, our daughters, and myself. Fever ridden, with no time left, we drove 700 miles east.

Merry Christmas.

When we arrived, I gazed at the home of my childhood with anticipation more akin to a dentist's chair than a glad celebration. I opened the door.

The scene inside was chaos—of the best kind. Mom and Dad sat in their comfortable armchairs near the fire, watching the kids swarm over a nine-foot tree, adding decorations in wild free-form.

"Oh, Mom." My daughters' eyes were enormous.

"Go on, we'll bring the bags in." But I was talking to myself. The girls had already joined the fray.

Brother Brian emerged from the kitchen, silver tinsel in his hand, on his sweater, and in his hair. His eyes shone as they had on Christmases long past. "They decorated me first," he laughed. "Isn't this a great tree? Cut it myself this morning."

Jeff and Betts burst through the door, pink-cheeked from the cold, groceries in tow. Jeff flashed his best Teddy Roosevelt grin at me. "Wait'll you see the goodies still in the car."

The children couldn't wait, and in a stampede of little feet, out they went, tumbling and shoving and laughing. Children's laughter is the most wonderful of music.

The two days before Christmas whirled by in grand prepara-tions—the ballet was enjoyed to the fullest extent; the decorations in our Cherry Hill neighborhood were admired; the house sparkled with golden bows Betts draped over the banister, and with stockings for all twenty of us that Janice hung by the chimney. My satin, velvet, and foil Father Christmas reigned benignly from the mantle.

We reenacted cherished traditions of my memory. The after-noon before Christmas, my sisters-in-law helped me bring out the good china, spread the French lace cloth, and set the tables with the Grand Baroque. At twilight we left for a poinsettia-decorated church, and returned to a feast, and a house once more redolent of turkey, evergreen, apples, and pumpkin pie.

The next morning ten children tumbled down the stairs to rip into Santa's munificence overflowing from the foyer into the living room.

"Look what I got," rang through the house, as they rushed to each adult in turn to show their goodies.

The adults watched the bacchanalia, and I knew we were all remembering other mornings like this.

Occasionally, we would glance at Mom and Dad. My father's gray complexion was tinged with rose. He leaned over, hugged Mom's waist and mouthed the words, "I love you." Mom's return smile and Dad's glow made them beautiful.

As the chaos subsided, Mom stood and called for silence. From the pocket of her housecoat, she pulled four envelopes. "Merry Christmas," she said, and handed one to each of my brothers and me.

Written inside my card was a message. "You cannot begin to understand the joy we feel in this gathering. Our family is the source of our greatest happiness. God bless you for this gift."

I caught my brother Brian peeking at me from over his card. His eyes were suspiciously red, and he grinned sheepishly, as did Jeff and Joey.

Irritation, pettiness, any complaints about how fairly we divided our "precious time" were transcended in the light of the happiness we had given to our parents and to our children. There may be a limit to time in this world of ours, but thank God, no limit to love.

—➤➤➤•◄◄◄—

Although this was the first Christmas gathering of the clan for more than a decade, family reunions have been held every summer on Cape Cod for the last twelve years. Everyone promises to continue the custom.

— FAMILY IS FOREVER —

WE ARE ALWAYS DELIGHTED TO HEAR FROM OUR READERS, especially if they would like to share *their* stories. Please write us with tributes, memories, anecdotes, and family traditions at:

Mary Pesaresi & Samantha Glen
P. O. Box 1405
Alpharetta, GA 30239-1405

Should your story be used in a future volume, you will be acknowledged and given credit. We look forward to learning about your families!

— CONTRIBUTING WRITERS —

"Beyond the Silence" is printed with permission of Michael Harr, 1996.

"Cycles of Life," "Listen . . . ," "Sittie's Hands," and "If Only I'd Told You I Loved You" are printed with permission of Linda Azar, 1996.

"The End of the Rainbow" is printed with permission of Sara Pesaresi, 1996.

"Grandma Left Us on a Monday" is printed with permission of Daniel James Cashmere, 1996.

"Her Only Coat" is printed with permission of Dawn Miller, 1996.

"I Remember Allison" is printed with permission of Shannon Elaine Denny, 1996.

"Irreplaceable" is printed with permission of Kenneth Smith, 1996.

"Life Support" is printed with permission of Theresa Mills, 1996.

"Life with Vava" and "Revelation" are printed with permission of Brian Baumann, 1996.

"The Miracle of Prayer" is printed with permission of Liz Kolshak, 1996.

"One in a Million" is printed with permission of Christy DeBoe Hicks, 1996.

"The Search" is printed with permission of D. J. Higo, 1996.

"Zebra Stripes" is printed with permission of Jennifer Shingleton, 1996.